Michael Sherlock is currently living in Birmingham, England and is of Irish background. He left school at 15 and went into silkscreen printing and commercial art as well as various other work, including painting and decorating.

He lived back in Ireland for a number of years before returning to Birmingham where he now lives.

MICHAEL SHERLOCK

Tales from the Clay Pipeman

AUSTIN MACAULEY PUBLISHERS™
LONDON • CAMBRIDGE • NEW YORK • SHARJAH

A CIP catalogue record for this title is available from the British Library.

ISBN 9781035872503 (Paperback)
ISBN 9781035872510 (ePub e-book)

www.austinmacauley.com

This Edition published 2024
First Published 2023
Austin Macauley Publishers Ltd®
1 Canada Square
Canary Wharf
London
E14 5AA

I dedicate this book to the memory of my dear sister, Ann Ashmore,
to whom I owe a debt of gratitude and who helped in putting into type
part of my early manuscript and for her encouragement.

I would like to thank my grandson, Thomas Sherlock, who generously gave his time in helping to arrange my final manuscript which I appreciated with gratitude.

Poems

Mr News Man 11

The Pig from the Fair 12

Bighead.com 13

The Dancing Chicken 14

Out of Time 15

Goodbye To Danny 16

New York Squatter 17

Butler of Bird Hall Keep 18

A Mirage 19

Storm the Dog 20

Newton Newton 21

Stage Coach Hill 22

Gypsy Joe and the Dancing Dog 23

Hiding in my Hood 24

New Feathered Bed 25

Kitty O'Leary 26

Lost Hand and the Desert Son 27

Sad Sam and Sorry Jane 28

Washing Machine Head 29

Sneezing Convention 30

Goodbye Sally Ann 31

A Frog Named Horus McGreen 32

Lady for Tea 33

Ballincrea Lady 35

A Drifter's Lament to his Girl 36

A Room without a View 37

A Year Ago 38

Answer the Phone 39

Apple Head Jack 40

Assistance Needed 41

Backward Pedal Bike 42

Bagman's Farewell 43

Bamboo Flute Player 44

Bed bug Sidney 45

Bellman Sam 46

Bertie Bow Street Singer 47

Billy the Bird 48

Birmingham Man 49

Black Birds' Choice 50

Blame the Cat 51

Blue Nose Don't Sneeze 52

Blue Rusty Coal Bucket 53

Cabbage Head Charlie 54

Careless Doug 55

Catwalk Queen 56

Chatter Box Harry 57

Class Asleep 58

Clay Pipe Winnie 59

Clean Sweep Motivator 60

Clock Watches Convention 61

Day Long Age 63

Dead Man's Wake 64

Dog's Tail Swipe 65

Dreamer Jack 66

Empty Chairs 67

Pleasantries Grudgingly Exchanged 68

Face in a Crowd 69

Faces Remembered 70

Fagan's About 71

Fast Cook 72

Fellow Traveller 73

Field Of Dreams 74

Find the Goose 75

Fourteen Not Seven 76

Freddy the Fly 77

Free Man 78

Gas Light Sally 79

Glasses in the Rain 80

Goodbye Old Joe Bones 81

Harry the Fish 82

Henry the House Mouse 83

Hopping Lady 84

In the Dog House 85

Jack's Lament 86

Joe the Hat Is Lost 87

Key for the Door for the Dog 88

King Tim Tack 90

Lady in a Bottle 91

Lamplighter Dan 92

Len the Shadow 93

Lime Bucket and Brush 94

Locked Down Charlie 95

London Club 96
Long Time Moving Son 97
Lost Dog 98
Lost in a Dream 99
Man and Bike at the Town Gate 100
Melonacther Road 101
Millers Farmyard Wall 102
Millie the Tap Dancer 103
Mirror Thoughts 104
Misty Blue Shoes 105
Moments 106
Moody Blues 107
Moon Shadow 108
Moonlight Shadows 109
Moonlight Shine 110
Music Man 111
My Rose Of Old Kentucky Town 112
Name On the Board 113
Needless Joe 114
Nosey Nancy 115
Old Dan the Joe 116
Old Jack the Bike 117
Old Joe Bones Has Gone 118
Old Sawdust Mill 119
Olive for Tea 120
One Night Stop in Ballyagran 121
Out of Sight 122
Peter Flea 123
Picture Photo 124
Pie Man Sam 125
Plastic Phone Anxiety 126
Ploughman Sidney 127
Poor Benny 128
Poor Man at the Door 129
Rag Man Black Bat 130
Rambling Round the Old Road 131
Rock Star Music Man 132

Sam and His Ham 133
Show Me 134
Shutters Down 135
Sidney Drover Tight Rope Walker 136
Someone's Daughter, Someone's Son 137
Someone's Son 138
Sorry John 139
Stone Cutter Jack 140
Sweet Harvest Jane 141
Ted at the Door 142
Teddy Freddy's Party 143
The Annual Brown Duck Race 144
The Bearded Mountain People 145
The Bell Rang 146
The Biscuit Boys 147
The Blue Goose Fair 148
The Cabbage Eater 149
The Donegal Fair 150
The Man From Clare 151
The Mildew Hut 152
The Millwheel Turns Again 153
The Old Road 154
The Open Road Festival 155
The Redundant Family Chair 156
The Reluctant Pig and Goose 157
The Shoemaker King 158
The Toothless Sailor 159
Too Many Years 160
Trail Dweller 161
Trumpet Blues 162
Upside Down Paper Reader 163
Where the Jacks 164
Who's in Who's Out 165
Wilson Picket 166
Wonder No More 167
Woodland Fair 168
Yellow Feather 169

Mr News Man

Hello Mr News man
Have you found an issue
Over something brewing
Gossip by the gossips
Stirring up the menu
Making accusations
Over exaggerations
Doubt on solid grounds
Don't let it bother me now
Take the road that's marked with pain
News is news and its bound to rain
Trouble in the night trouble in the day
Awake asleep it's still the same
It's raining cats and dogs
It's raining catch the news
There's something in the air,
It happened yesterday.

The Pig from the Fair

Master McSue he had one pig to the fair one day went they,
Five guineas I'll take if you care to wait while my pig and I take tea,
And tea did they have at the pitman's fair taken with a pigs Farewell,
Now Master McSue he has no pig no more to the fair will go,
Not that he cared for the tea at the fair, but the pig where left a tear,
A pig man named Pat the other McCarl bought the tea drinking pig at the fair,
Five guineas they paid and had to wait while McSue and his pig took tea,
The pig he died of broken heart a week and day from the fair,
The pig man named Pat the other McCarl wept more tears than McSue at the fair,
Five guineas they lost five guineas had gone for a heart broken pig from the fair,
A butcher McSam with a glee in his eyes cared nothing for the pig men's demise,
Pig meat for sale that's all he could see,
With his hand on his heart and a wink and a smile he offered to take
Their pig off their hands,
No guineas would he pay no guineas would he give for a lifeless pig from the fair,
The pig man named Pat the other McCarl agreed with heartfelt regret,
Five guineas they lost a pound of sausage they gained from butcher McSam's
generous heart?

Bighead.com

Bighead.com
Full of answers
First with hands up
Show off showman
Jumps the queue
With a crossword puzzle finished first
For a coffee break
Bighead.com
What's the problem? Not his fault
Clever sod
Computer expert
Self-taught surfer on the web
With the other prats,
Bighead.com
Serial bookworm
Reads a book on his coffee break
Got no time for small time banter
Reads the Times while he eats his fudge,
Bighead.com
Office turnoff
Big time pillock
On his phone
Boring know all
First to leave the office his work done,
So clear off go home and leave us alone,
Bighead.com Office turnoff.

The Dancing Chicken

The fox and the ferret,
Were not good friends,
On account of the dancing chicken,
Who blamed each other late at night,
While the chicken danced the polka,
Concern had grown between them both,
Outside the wiry coop,
With the moon looking on, the owl not impressed,
With the fox and the ferrets concern,
The chicken meanwhile continued to dance
A hornpipe with the duck and the goose,
Who could imagined on a bright starlit night
Inside and outside the coop
A foxtrot for the fox, a jig for the ferret,
Would solved the problem for both,
"Let us in so we can dance a fine jig or two,"
Cried the ferret in agreement with the fox,
The chicken he knew he could dance a fine jig
Without the fox or the chicken in tow,
Who were there to dance for a chicken or two,
By the light of the silvery moon,
So they all danced away by the light of the moon,
Until the sun rose to greet the new day,
The fox and the ferret have gone home to bed
Without a chicken to put in there bread,
And back again for night at the dance for a chicken
Or two maybe.
Said the angry fox to the sleeping ferret "I don't like
Chickens who dance" "only to eat," came a ferrets
Reply asleep till the light of the moon.

Out of Time

Look at you you walk to the other side,
You drop your head close your eyes
It's nothing to do with you,
Look at me I am still on the other side,
I comb my hair stand and stare,
It's nothing to do with me,

It's life's old story it happen to me,
Now it's happening to you,

Look at us we crossed to the other side,
We close our eyes drop our heads,
Like strangers from out of time,
Look at us we pass to the other side,
We don't look back or stand and stare,
Just faded out of sight,

It's life's old story it happen to me,
Now it's happen to you.

Goodbye To Danny

Danny died in the first world war,
Twenty one years and all that time,
Drank no beer, drank no wine,
Stayed with his mother and her two stray dogs,
His Father died in the old Boar war,
By a snipers bullet he fell stone dead,
Danny rode his Fathers bike,
And smoked his pipe in the old bike shed,
Courted one girl who said goodbye,
And found another when he went to war,
Over the top when the whistle blew his bayonet at the ready.
And a field gun blew his young head right away,
Danny died in the First World War twenty-one years and all that time,
In the battle field without saying goodbye.

New York Squatter

I'm a subway squatter in New York town
I'm feeling better right now
Met a man in the street today
He turned his head and walked away
The lady and the parrot and her blue brown hair
That's okay her parrot would say
Funny what people have to say
Living in a time that has no time
But I'm happy that way I'm happy to say
Slept all night without a light
Thought I was walking on air
My girlfriend said her name was Jane
I think it's going to rain
Her shoes are lose her hair is grey
That's okay I happen to say
Funny what people have to say
Living in a time that has no time
But I'm happy that way
I'm happy to say
The man in the box with his bottle of brown
Said his feet are lost and his heads not there
He waved goodbye to his sally Anne
His graffiti picture on the subway wall
The man in the corner with his nose turned blue
He's hiding in his hood and he's not there
Funny what people have to say
living in a time that has no time
But I'm happy that way I'm happy to say
Were subway squatters in New York town
Were feeling better right now
What day is it today has yesterday gone?
Somewhere over the rainbow you'll find us
Shouted Jane to herself that's okay she's happy to say
Funny what people have to say living in a time that has no time
Were subway squatters in New York town.

Butler of Bird Hall Keep

Don't drink the pigeon water,
Young man of twenty-one,
Wake up and be glad,
You have chosen to stay at Bird Hall keep,
Reflect your bright imagination,
Remove your bitterness,
Corruption unchecked,
May undo your ambition,
Hardly encouraging temporary mishap,
Mountains without tops,
Are part of life's enduring possibilities,
Hold together say goodbye to yesterday,
Smile and be free to cry out,
Without self conscience observations,
Resume your post,
Hold fast and stand firm,
And make way for the twenty-first butler,
Of Bird Hall keep.

A Mirage

Dust me down on the trail I came
Pretty lady you're sure to stay
Wipe my brow with your nut brown hair and a smile from your desert blue
eyes
A drink from your fresh water well
Would make my parched mouth straight again
From the heat of the cruel desert sun
Those shifting sands took me out of shape
I'm here but I'm not all there
Pretty lady stay a while on this journey Mans retreat
Conceal maybe a sandstorm dream
Pretty lady my desert lady please stay a while
Until the camels arrive and I will say goodbye
To you my lady with your desert blue eyes and your nut brown hair.

Storm the Dog

Storm on the wall
Himself proud upright nose activated
Tail gently swishing away at the persistent summer fly
Himself with careful respectful caution
Dismounts from grandmothers or great grandmother's basket filled bike
Storm knew the bike was old
Like the old pedal man
Who would slowly pass him bye
With careful judgement and respect for him on the wall
The master at the door with his clay pipe in hand waved good day
To himself a smile or two was exchanged
To reassure storm a friend is passing by
Not a foe he had hoped for
Yet pedal man always offered storm a piece of broken chocolate
As a peace offering which he expected
With a half a wag of a storm dogs tail
And pedal man slowly pedalled into the distance with a nervous whistle
Relieved careful not to look back for obvious reasons
Storm remained on the wall
Watching the unnoticed pedal man fading into the distance
Until he spotted and unconcerned rabbit passing by
Who showed him no respect
Why should I thought the rabbit to himself
Storm is only a storm in a teacup
All bark too lazy to chase his own tail
Storm knew Billy rabbit was a pain in his butt
Showing him little concern or respect

Sooner or later he hoped Kenny fox would take care of Billy rabbit
without too much fuss
So storm could continue to be a Storm cloud
To those unfortunate who found him intimidating
To the good pleasure of his master
Who knew storm was all bark.

Newton Newton

An apple fell from the tree today
And hit me on the head
I told my Mommy I never cried
When the apple fell on my head
My girlfriend's boyfriend
Said okay
When the apple fell on my head
Newton Newton
It's not your fault
When the apple fell on my head
My dog named Bark
With a leap of surprise
Caught the apple
That fell from my head
My cat named Milk
Dropped his mouse from his mouth
With the shock
When the apple fell on my head
Newton Newton
It's not your fault
When the apple fell on my head
The mouse was glad
The apple fell on my head
As he scarpered away
With some haste
The man on his bike with a feather in his hat
And a coat signed apples for sale
Thought it funny
When the apple fell on my head.

Stage Coach Hill

It was a wet and dreary night
The wild wind creeping round stage coach hill
Where the last highway man disappeared with lady Blackmore and her loyal
staff with coach and horses
Mystery many years have passed
Stage coach hill has kept its secret
Some would say the witch of the robin tree changed them all into faceless stones
Where are they now?
Who knows only the robin of stage coach hill
And the faceless stones.

Gypsy Joe and the Dancing Dog

Gypsy Joe played his flute
While his dog danced the wondering horn pipe
Such elegance and poise from a dancing dog
With his gypsy Joe on the flute
The crowd gathered round
Delighted to watch the performance
That filled them with good cheer
A call to join the dance with the dog
While his gypsy Joe continued to play
His rendition
Of the wonderful wondering hornpipe
And they all danced until the moon came up
And gypsy Joe and his dog went on their way
To play again and dance the wondering hornpipe
As they faded out sight.

Hiding in my Hood

I'm hiding in my hood; I'm hiding in my hood
Looking kind of bad
I'm lying in my bed, thinking in my head
My hood is on my head my teddy doesn't speak
The walls are caving in the mirror tells me lies
I'm speaking to myself my girlfriends gone to Spain
Her boyfriend's coming back
My job is on the line I'm first in and first out
My school had let me go and told me I'm not welcome back
Hide your face my Nan said so I hid my face in my old man's coat
I feel okay in the dark
People side step and body swerve away from me
They are frightened of me and I'm frightened of them
The police constantly stop me and ask to see my head
I say which head? mine or teddies?
When they look at my head they say you look better in your hood
I agree and so does teddy
I am hiding in my hood I am hiding in my hood
I am feeling kind of bad.

New Feathered Bed

I'm home today without a care,
With my brand new feathered bed,
And out will go old rusty springs that tore my arse to shreds,
What changed my mind I cannot hide a wife of two days old,
Who refused to lie on old rusty springs and listen to its nightmare sounds,
Yet I must confess with some regret I miss old rusty springs,
For forty years without a wife my bachelors bed held out,
Handed down from father to son and grandfather's pride and joy,
History now past and gone retired to some scrap yard retreat,
And it's goodbye farewell to old rusty springs and my bachelor's life farewell,
And hello to my wife of two days old and my brand new feathered bed.

Kitty O'Leary

Kitty O'Leary, met a strange man,
On the road to the pig man's fair,
Can you dance a fine jig with a man
From Clare by the light of the silvery moon,
With my fiddle and pig, and a goose on the loose,
And a comb for my blue brown hair,
Indeed you are a strange man with your fiddle and pig
And a goose on the loose on the way to the pig man's fair
To dance a fine jig with my wellie boots on,
Could damage your blue suede shoes,
Worry not my dear with your nut brown hair,
And my pony tail to match,
You're the right girl for a man from Clare,
To dance by the light of the moon,
With your wellie boots on
And my blue suede shoes
And a fiddle without bending my the bow,
So Kitty O'Leary danced a fine jig
With the man and his pig from Clare
And the goose on the loose came to
Join in the fun on the road to the pig mans fair
And they danced all night until the sun came up
Then parted without saying a word
And so ends the tail of the man from Clare,
With his fiddle pig and goose,
o Leary went back to her worried husband,
who wondered what the fuss was about
On the road to the pig man's fair.

Lost Hand and the Desert Son

Your face is dusty
Worn out with cracks
A true desert rat
A lifelong sandman
A Bedouin trail blazer
Who made his home in the desert sand
Forty years lived on scorpions and desert moles
Forgot who he was
What year he lived in
The long lost son of Henry the hand
Who lost his hand in his butchers shop
Don't waste the hand he told his son
So he put his hand through the sausage grinder
Mixed in with the sausage mix
Sent his son to deliver the sausages
Who never came back
Years after he wrote a book about his Fathers hand and life in the desert sand.

Sad Sam and Sorry Jane

Sad Sam met Sorry Jane
To dance a sorrowful tango
A festival of dance held once a year
For all the sad and sorrowful people
Who gathered from all parts
Encouraged to come along and join the depressive atmosphere
And dance to the out of tune
Unpopular band
Called the Sons of Tears
Sad Sam and Sorry Jane
Have one thing in common
They're both Sad and Sorry
Like everyone else they have come not to enjoy the dance
But to feel no longer alone
The top prize is not the best dancer
It's the saddest face
Sad Sam and Sorry Jane
Are this year's winners
Top prize is two weeks in a psychiatric hospital of their choice.

Washing Machine Head

Your spinning around my washing machine head,
The world in a mess and I'm still in bed,
Did you say meet me tomorrow
Has yesterday gone,
The cats at the door, the dogs round the bend,
Can't find my feet to take off my shoes,
Has breakfast finished my teas gone cold
I'm out bed and laughing out loud,
It's all good fun when you're not so young.
Your spinning around my washing machine head,
My shirt needs ironing, my hairs in a mess,
My socks are on teddy and his in my bed
Can't wake him or call him his dreaming his dead
My dog needs feeding and the cats on the phone
I'm feeling I'm here but I'm not all there,
Remind me to meet you what day did you say
Tomorrow or yesterday that seems okay.
Your spinning around my washing machine head,
The curtains are opened the moon gone to bed
I'm happy I'm smiling I think I'm half crying
With my book and pencil I'm ready for bed,
My cat gone asleep the dogs half awake,
I'm hungry and thirsty my mouse has gone crazy,
Ring me tomorrow when the phones on the hook
So I can remember if I'm not on the moon
Good night till tomorrow I'm thinking of you
when tea and coffee will be served for two
Don't bother to call me I'll be there at two,
So you can spin around with my washing machine head.

Sneezing Convention

Jack the Nose thought he would be late for the annual sneezing convention
Which takes place in June or July
Depending on the high level of pollen in the air
Necessary for quality sneezing
Jack the Nose had been banned, disqualified for a year
found to have had snuff up his nose before the competition to enhance sneezing
He knows he will never be able to win
Without his trusted box of snuff
He knows all of the contestants will have their noses tested for tell-tale signs of
brown clinkers up their noses
No hiccupping
Or whistling
False teeth must be removed while sneezing
Hearing aids must also be removed while sneezing
Rules must be kept
Jack the Nose doesn't care it's about not taking part this year
With his likeminded sneezing friends after the competition is finished there is a free
and easy sneezing party for all
Plus free snuff for all and Jack the Nose is included
Footnote with much high sneezing going on the emergency services had to be called
people living outside the convention area reported hearing laud noises
Coming from inside the convention centre.

Goodbye Sally Ann

Said goodbye to Sally Ann
Walked a mile took my time
Went to the valley of the stone pit mine
Drank some wine, cleared my mind
Sally Ann it's not your fault
We could've done better if we had more time to change our minds
That's not true we had more time
To start again and not look back
I'm travelling light with no regrets
When I said goodbye to Sally Ann
And the stone pit mine
Where I drank some wine and cleared my mind.

A Frog Named Horus McGreen

A man named Jack with his brown hair-ed dog
Met a frog named Horus McGreen
Who stood on a leaf by a green water brook
Who spoke better English than Jack or his brown haired dog
Where did you learn such elegant words for a frog near a green
water brook with a name Horus McGreen
Frogs school where-learnt such words to speak
That makes sense to you and your brown haired dog
So they spent the day listening to Horus McGreen
And they agreed-to meet again and learn from-the wise-talking frog
And the man named Jack with his brown haired dog
learnt to speak better English than their friends or foes
Thanks to their friend Horus McGreen the wise talking green frog
who stood-on-leaf by a green water brook

Lady for Tea

She's over the top,
She's coming to tea,
The music is playing,
The cats on the fence,
My socks have gone missing,
My mind's in a mess,
The posh Lady Sarah
She's coming to tea.

She's over the top,
She coming to tea,
What time did she call me
Or leave me a note,
The barking dogs helped me
To gather my thoughts,
The posh Lady Sarah
She's coming to tea.

She's over the top
She coming to tea,
What day is tomorrow
Has yesterday gone,
My socks are still missing,
My hair in a mess
I'm shaking all over
My wall clock has stopped,
The posh Lady Sarah

She's coming to tea,
She's over the top
She's coming to tea,
My mouse has arrived with my comb and my socks,
My mirror is cracked two faces I see,
Which one is mine the other one's not,
The table is ready my dog has helped out,
And where are the cups with their handles still on,
Somewhere over the rainbow said my cat on his phone,
The posh Lady Sarah
She's coming to tea,

Knock Knock Knock,
Who opened the door,
Not me said the dog the cat or my mouse,
Her voice we hear she's over the top,
The posh Lady Sarah
Has arrived for tea.

Ballincrea Lady

In a bottle stands a lady near the town of Ballincrea,
How she got there ask the sailor,
who found her in the sea,
In a bottle he will tell you,
Stood a lady small and fair,
So the sailor took the bottle to his home in Ballincrea,
If you ask him where his house is and the lady small and fair,
He will tell you in a bottle,
Near the town of Ballincrea.

A Drifter's Lament to his Girl

No time left to say goodbye
Dear maid my heart's desire
I'm on my way to some where's end
And called to say a quiet farewell
To you dear maid near the parting gate
With gifts of love daisy chains and buttercup smiles
To end our time with parting tears
Dear maid dear maid my summer love
You're out of sight
I miss you most near the parting gate
Where we met and loved in calm summer days
With thoughts gathered shared with hope to meet again
at the parting gate on our journey's end.

A Room without a View

Who lives in a room without a view
Or cat with a two times tail
On the wall hangs a picture of himself upsides down
With a tooth that had not been cleaned since it first appeared in his open mouth
Over in the corner of his dust covered room
Stands a pair of odd matching shoes
Which only fit his feet when he fails to cut his nails
A chair a table a bowl of cold soup
A crust of bread
Now marinated by the house ants
Who were not invited
Are welcomed to stay anyway
Whose complaining when life is so hard from his head to his toes
Head stands on a concrete floor
Helps his brain from closing down
And his house ants agreed, makes sense to them
So does his cat with his two times tail
Agrees to disagree or understand without complaining
With his head on the concrete floor

A Year Ago

You were just a year ago
A painted picture on the wall
Light shades colours never fade
Darkness covers your goodbye eyes
Memories remain
A year has passed
No long road back
Wind rain tapping on the window pane
Your voice I hear in long winter nights
Dreams fade return never the same
Stand or sit wake or sleep
Laugh sometimes without tears
Take the picture off the wall
Time to let go
Dry your eyes move on
Remember she was just a year ago
And you were just a year ago
Goodbye picture on the wall
Where only your memories linger on

Answer the Phone

Answer the phone the poor man said
To his friend named Peg the leg near the river bend
That's fine said Peg the leg when he answered the phone
Phone me back when you can
Who rang the poor man said to Peg the leg near the river bend
A man with a dog and a hat made of gold
Replied the Peg the leg near the river bend
Okay that's fine without casting a thought a smile
Or moving his lips
So let us dance to the Woodpeckers tree top tap
It makes sense to answer the phone
When you have no phone
It's easier that way the poor man agreed
As they danced around the river bend and back again
To the tap of the Woodpeckers tap

Apple Head Jack

Apple Head Jack the apple eating king
Hopes to win again the eagerly awaited annual apple eating competition which takes
place once a year during the apple picking season
Open only to competitors who can consume three dozen apples per hour
The competition is two hours long the competitor who can eat the most apples
Is declared the winner
The prize for the winner is taken to emergency private health care hospital of
 choice to relive chronic stomach pain expenses paid by the Apple Tree Club
If the winner survives he will be booked in to a private nursing home to recover
When better back to the club house for the Apple Tree presentation cup for the
winner with a basket of the best fresh green apples
 All the runners up who have survived a bag of red and green apples each
And so ends another successful annual apple eating competition enjoyed by all
Even the chronic pain survivors' declare it was worth it as they declaring no gain
without pain and have already signed up for next years apple eating competition
Apple Head Jack is still the apple eaten King even after many serious stomach
Operations he will be back again next year to defend his title against the advice of
doctors and family not so the Apple Tree Committee who value Apple Head Jack as
their biggest assist for crowed pulling and ticket sales hoping we were all there when
Apple Head Jack the greatest of all apple head eaters would finely say goodbye to his
stomach and bury him before he turned into cider
That was Apple Head Jacks last nightmare dream and retired soon after also the
Apple Tree club closed due to lack of support plus a bad year for apple growers.

Assistance Needed

Assistance needed to complete my journey
The sidewalks long
It's short when you walk it
I'm back where I started from I passed this way
Excuse my observation excuse my observation
For a second I noticed you then you were gone
Backwards and forwards
Forwards and backwards
Flowing with the crowd, I'm lost in time
Thinking to myself it's hard to cry
Look at the man behind the face
Look at the man behind the face
It's time for him to cry
When I am going forward am I going backwards
I asked a man in the street today which way to go
follow your nose Sir the blind man said that's the way to go
Backwards and forwards
Forwards and backwards
Flowing with the crowd I am lost in time
Look at the man inside his hood his not smiling his only brooding said the man in
the street with a feather in his hat
If I am going forward am I going backwards if I am going backwards am I going
forwards
Which way to go is the right way that's the way to go
Not the other way said the man in the hood to the feathered hat man.

Backward Pedal Bike

Pedal man could only ride his bike backwards not foreword
Strange said the man with his pipe upside down
And the lady walking sidewards with her pram
Not so strange said pedal man it's easy than going foreword
To the other man walking backwards and the police man claiming up the ladder to
get a better view who found the peddle mans bike unusual
Many the towns folk where walking on their hands and cars driving backwards
 Passer's by found pedal man and the town folk strange not so pedal man who lived
in the town and found the town folk not unusual
You can find this town on the map if you turn it upside down.

Bagman's Farewell

The old park bench man is dead
He has gone without a mildew farewell
Yes laid out on his cold death bench slab
Surrounded by his beloved carrier bags
Full of carrier bags
Leaving them to whom will throw them into the nearest skip
Old park bench man
Your memories are all gone with a woodpecker's farewell
So sing along with a squirrel's nut
Or dance a bench or two
And he who stood and sat with him
His cold shadow in the rain
Will remember nothing
Just a faded memory in the rain
For a bagman's farewell.

Bamboo Flute Player

The street man played
On his home made bamboo flute
To the delight of the good morning crowed
Who listened and danced to his foot tapping blues
Played on his bamboo flute
After he had finished he sang his rendition of his old time bamboo blues
And waved goodbye to the crowed as he drifted out of sight to the tune of his
foot tapping blues played on his home made bamboo flute

Bed bug Sidney

Bed bug Sidney the love bite king and his friends are not sleeping over tonight they will be busy
Only the bed people will be sleeping over
By the time love bite Sidney and his friends are finished with them they will be trying to sleep under the bed
Love bite Sidney and friends find the bed people unsociable when they have to follow them under the bed especially when bed bug Sidney and friends are only trying to be sociable buy giving the bed people plenty of love bites
Bed bug Sidney and friends consider themselves physical trainers giving the bed people plenty of exercise as they call it their night time gym
The bed people call it their worst nightmare stressed out without a good night sleep
Bed bug Sidney and friends have finished with the bed peoples night time work out so watch out bed people more love bites exercises when love bite Sidney and friends return after their own day time sleep over.

Bellman Sam

Bellman Sam
Rang his bell
And found he could not stop
He went to the doctor
For help if he could
And found Dr Bell quite helpful
Who directed him to the bell ringers club
Where he can ring his bell in comfort.

Bertie Bow Street Singer

Come gather around and listen to the new market street singer
Who can sing through his mouth nose and ear's each with their own distinguish
sound they can all sing together in harmony
With plenty of songs Bertie Bow can keep the crowd clapping dancing joining in
with his songs
His nose would sing a few songs also his ear's and Bertie Bow himself would also sing
a few songs of his own with so many parts of head taking part in the performance
the new market street singer never seemed to get tired with so much help from his
head parts
When asked how he is able to sing through his nose ears and mouth altogether in
harmony he said he can only speak for his mouth you will have to ask his nose and
ears each separately what an answer from this very unusual three part head singer
Sing on Bertie Bow the new market street singer.

Billy the Bird

Billy the bird woke from a dream
Thought he could fly like a bird
High up in the sky
And out of the window he launched himself
One bright sunny morn
Like a bird flapping his arms
On the high wind and low wind
What has become of Billy the Bird
You may ask or not
Nobody knows only Billy himself
After he woke from his bird like dream.

Birmingham Man

A well known man from Birmingham
Whose name was Sammy the Man
Who drank from a can
Bought a pan
To cook without burning his ham
He lived in a house without any doors
Windows without any glass
With a cat and a dog, a fish for a friend
And a mouse who came through the open front door
And they all lived together helping Sammy the Man eat his ham from his pan.

Black Birds' Choice

Which way will the blackbird fly?
When the dark clouds cover the sky
Towards the trees near the river bend
Or the house near the old village pump
To the old mill house he could fly just south
From the bridge where he stands to watch
There's a fisher mans hut just up in front
Now covered in moss and rot
In the roof of the hut he has stayed to rest
From the wind that blows to the south
Which way will he fly Is a blackbirds choice
From the bridge where he stands to watch.

Blame the Cat

The man at the door
With his bike and dog
His wife at the door with the rabbit
The key is lost who lost the key
Each looked at one another with malice
Their cat at the door they agree with relish and spite
Lost the key they discerned mischievous they looked with serious concern without
hindrance or pleasure they displayed
The cat can take the blame truly claimed without question or doubt in their minds
The man at the door with his bike and dog found the key in his overcoat pocket no
apologies to the cat or an extra bowl of milk the cat took the blame and the wife and
the rabbit agreed
And the man at the door with dog bike wife and rabbit thanked the cat for taking the
blame without an extra bowl of milk not that the cat cared as he had his own spare
key so while they were all out he helped himself to the milk
Poor cat they all thought it's his own fault for taking the blame and the cat agreed
with his belly full of milk with a poor cat's meow.

Blue Nose Don't Sneeze

Blue nose don't hide your face
Your nose is yours and not your friends
They don't have a hotter like yours
That's not your fault
Blue nose blue nose
Please warn your friends
To run for cover and hide their heads
A blue nose sneeze could wake the dead
Its earth quake sound could turn your furniture upside down
So hoot and toot your trumpet sound
Before you blow out of control
And go and join the blue nose club
Who understands your trumpet sound
Don't leave your friends without a warning
Blue nose blue nose please don't sneeze.

Blue Rusty Coal Bucket

The old blue rusty coal bucket
Half covered in grey wet sand
Left forgotten
Attention diverted
Something better elsewhere
Mothers inherited coal bucket
Handed down through family
Proudly handed to trusted son
Inwardly screams not again
Unhappy at school
Occupied by coal bucket thoughts
Collector of lonely sea coal
A way of life
A pat on the back for a full bucket
Extra bread and jam in grandfather's day
Pie and chips for grandson
Well done son
You're a true sea coal collector

Cabbage Head Charlie

Cabbage head Charlie has been shopping for more cabbage heads
To make new cabbage leaf clothes for his birthday party
All his cabbage leaf family and friends are coming
All dressed in their new designer cabbage leaf outfits
And plenty of boiled cabbage will be served and eaten by all
And Charlie knows they will all be up for second helpings
And happy birthday to Charlie will be sung by all
And presents of cabbage heads will be given to him
Thanking him for a great cabbage party
And they all danced and sang their cabbage leaf rock songs
And after the dance a sad song was sung
I lost my love to a carrot head eater
Which reminded Charlie of his own lost love to a turnip head eater
And so ends Charlie's cabbage leaf birthday party
Enjoyed by all
And Charlie offered them one more bowl of boiled cabbage before they departed
And with a resounding yes they all got stuck into another bowl of Charlie's boiled
cabbage
And they all sang for Charlie
For he's a jolly good fellow
As they waved him goodbye
After a wonderful cabbage head party enjoyed by all.

Careless Doug

Careless Doug the baker man's son
Lost his teeth while mixing his doe
Into the oven bread to bake
Never again did he find his teeth
Dan Joe the eye bought some bread from the baker man's son
With a look of surprise he found Doug's teeth
Which fitted his gum less gums like a treat
Dan Joe the eye never told careless Doug he found his teeth in his the bread only to
say with a smile the best bread ever.

Catwalk Queen

Assert yourself
Hide your personality
Not someone else's personality
Catwalk queen of the rolling tar boat song
Escape into another outfit
Stand still and don't watch others
Hold your head don't listen to your feet
They will only walk back and forth if you let them
Hold tight your pose
Who for Mr Nobody
Only yourself
Without notice
Who cares not your shoes
They only need changing
So be careful not to smile
On the catwalk
Or you'll blow their minds
And their wallets
That makes no sense to you or them
So Catwalk Queen go for it strut your stuff make them notice you
With or without their glasses or their monocle heads.

Chatter Box Harry

Chatter box Harry could never stop talking
About something or nothing until his teeth fell out
And his gums could not chatter
His teeth continued to chatter and banter poor Harry had to listen to its
Mindless jabber that made no sense to Harry or his gums
Until Harry woke from his empty gums nightmare and found his teeth were back in
his head
Chatter box Harry never stopped talking but is careful to give his chatter box gums
a brake next time it may not be a dream but real which made poor Harry nervous
about meeting his nightmare teeth again and listen to its mindless jabber and banter
that made no sense to Harry his gums or his nightmare teeth.

Class Asleep

Class ready all in who's out who's not awake
Who's late not us shouted the whole class
Sir stood up from his old pine chair red face blood shot eyes hand shacking
Pointing to the unclean black board with his warn out black thorn cane
Cracking voice loud not clear called out
Are any of you awake yet or still asleep it's not a nursery
Wake up stand up sit down
Stop smiling smirking at each other you don't deserve to smile any of you
With that Sir sat down and fell fast asleep as he does every day until home time
And all the class fell asleep until the bell rang for home time
Sir wake up shouts who's late again
Time to go home Sir Oh class dismiss hope you remembered what you have learned today
Dreams are your homework.

Clay Pipe Winnie

Clay Pipe Winnie smoked her clay pipe outside her woodland mildew home
Content within herself after making another of her favourite tea leaf tobacco
Mix for her clay pipe refill dried out tea leaves after her last mug of tea
And smile she may if you could only see her face with the smoke and steam
Coming from her brown stained clay pipe like an out of controlled steam engine
Each puff gives way to another bout of uncontrolled coughing and choking
That leaves poor Winnie in a state of total confusion and panic with her lungs
crying out once again stop in the name of your tea leaf tobacco mix you are
mugging my lungs
Winnie is in denial never blames her beloved tea leaf tobacco mix for her lungs
demise believing the smoke and the steam coming from her clay pipe is
keeping her lungs clear her coughing and choking she feels is all part of a
unique experience of dried out tea leaf tobacco mix can give which makes clay
pipe smoking different from any other form of smoke breathing not that her
lungs would be in agreement with her tea leaf stained tobacco thoughts
Winnie is a proud member of the clay pipe tea leaf drinking woodland club
Who meet once a year to commiserate with each other and share the sad loss
of many of their departed tea leaf clay pipe smoking loyal friends whose lungs
were buried before them and a show of remembrance they are not forgotten
with a demonstration of puffing choking coughing their clay pipes in full burn
with their lungs gasping for air and they all agreed their departed friends
would have been proud of the tribute they all paid to them not so their lungs.

Clean Sweep Motivator

Hold fast your clean sweep arm
Make your mind up Mr Broom motivator
Your slow not fast disposition
Guide your habits to promote your imposing Ideas
Happy not sad
Time to think
Future tomorrow
Always today
Clean sweep Mr friendly man
Rehabilitate your main sweep arms not your head
Redundant broom promotes honour
With new broom
Thankful resentment played out
Without notice
Private hostility for own benefit
Engage in main office block corridor
Sweep through the day Sweep through the week
Turn up your personal head music that sweeps through your mind
Then hold fast your clean sweep arm Mr Broom motivator.

Clock Watches Convention

Clock watches convention hardly a clock seat empty
Or a cat's whisker for a fine tuned clock
The anthem rang out
Watches checked
Clocks watched
Wait for the chimes
Eyes in overdrive
Loud cheer
First clock cuckoo out
First passed the winning post
Move out now
For the first tea break
Shake hands
Watch the clocks for return
If late report to the clock master
Time deducted until the next tea break
Full day clock watching
Not fun
Serious business
Workshop for obsessive clock watching problems
Unable to watch clocks at the work place when busy
Clocking out my course concerns if the clocks are fast or slow
Bus late or early causes problems for time clock watchers
Car fails to start
May cause a nerves breakdown along with their car
Clock watches are nice people with their tick tock heads which keeps them ticking
over
Sleep is an inconvenience for clock watchers
They call it a clock watchers blackout for obvious reasons
All clock head problems are helped at the clock watchers
Convention workshops have their own clock watchers therapists
Who themselves are clock watcher have adjusted their tick tock heads to help others
to have some normal tick tock in their Cuckoo heads
The Convention closes with their national anthem the chimes
Of Big Ben
The watchers agreed It was another successful Convention they all left with smiles
and handshakes to meet again next year
They all went on their way with a great convention high ringing in their cuckoo
heads and ears.Dancing Lillie

Dancing Lillie the gum tree dancing Queen
First on the floor with her bubbly gum chew
Fast or slow with a bubbly or two
Keeps her in step with her up down chew
Gum tree night spot the place to be
Lillie is the Queen of the gum tree floor
The main event and high light of night the first shoes to stick fast to the gum
Tree floor wins the top prize a year's supply of sticky gum
Not surprising Lillie wins again the runners up have to spend time prising her
chewing gum shoes off the gum tree floor
The night ends with great fun and good cheer
As Lillie leads all her friends in prising each other's shoes off the bubbly gum floor

Day Long Age

Long ago in day long age,
Timeless seasons changing,
I dreamt of time that would come back,
To me that life was changing,
To free me then from hour long toil,
And time to spend worth changing,
And free I felt from time to time,
But that was never lasting,
And so from there it's still the same,
To see that I was changing,
And now I find that time I have,
Old age limits changing,
And all I have is day long dreams,
For me their never changing.

Dead Man's Wake

It's cold said he in his blue bare feet
Shoes and socks sold for a can or two
Oh dear what a mess to barter your foot ware for a can or two to ease the shakes from
the beat of factory stamping machines
As he beds himself down on his cardboard matt behind the factory skip
Only the old night time rat foraging around to remind him his not alone
An all weather man a journeyman man of the open road freedom he calls it
Not behind the factory skip until the juice of the barley kicks in to ease his sakes
After awhile he must find another skip before the morning jobbers arrive
He is in luck finds another skip and a dead man who left his bag of cans and a half
bottle of whiskey shoes and socks to match his blue feet and anything else he could
find on the dead man's corpse happy and sad that's how he felt as he raised his can
for a dead man's wake.

Dog's Tail Swipe

Alone without a dogs tail swipe
On a bench without a light
A thought that makes no sense
To an ear that hears no sound
Or catch a breath on the night time air
Where dreams fade without recall
And who would notice or care
Or look twice at a journey man on a derelict bench
Only those thoughts would fade in and out by those who pass him by
And disrupt their night time thinking
And they turn without concern
Alone to shiver until the morning dew
While his own thoughts pass him by
To face another day until his night time fades away.

Dreamer Jack

Old Time Dreamer Jack
Can travel anywhere without leaving his house
No on line bookings or phone calls needed
Boats trains planes always on time
No customs to check in no passport required or holiday bags
Travelling light on a dreamers flight
No need for food or drinks just close his eyes and away he goes
He can choose any holiday destination any hour day or night a real dreamer is Jack
even to the moon and back without a space ship
When he wakes from his dream he thinks he has a sun tan he even joined the
dreamers all time travel club anytime day or night always on their travels
They all share their travel dreams with each other
Time wasters procrastinators day dreamers drop outs are not welcome at the
dreamers travel club as the club is very careful who they except as new members a
letter from there psychiatrist or dream therapist would be required and interview
with one of the committee members of the dream travel club and finally the
chairman who happens to be old time dreamer Jack
Will take a decision to except a new member or not if successful all the dreamers will
gather around the new dreamer to welcome him or her to the dreamers club to share
their first travel dreams
Then they will all go back to their homes to get ready to prepare for their next night
time or day time travel dreams no worry' s about Mosquitoes only bed bugs that
might cause flight turbulence
Old time dreamer Jack is already in holiday dream land waves goodbye as he
fastening up his sleep belt and away he goes.

Empty Chairs

Empty chairs people disappeared somewhere
Separated to make their own way
Brief casual comments maybe
Common mutual banter shared
Exchanged with agreeing nods
Pull the curtain of life over their heads
Maybe they will change their coffee drinking minds
A spoonful of sugar may help
Might wake them up
Time to get up
And walk a crooked mile
Or two on a rainy day
Without their umbrellas
And back again coffee break over
People returning to empty chairs
Someone talking who is listening
No one they are all talking at once
Silence lost for words
And all the people say goodbye to each other and their empty chairs.

Pleasantries Grudgingly Exchanged

Pleasantries were exchanged grudgingly,
The atmosphere cold teeth gritting was the order of the day,
Resentments practiced, envy controlled with smiles that would
Frighten any ghost away,
The only thing they all had in common was issues against each other,
The only relive they found was twitting texting and biting their nails
They were the in crowd out crowd upside down crowd out of control crowd you
would find them anywhere without looking,
Any time any moment anywhere that's where you would find them
They all look the same talk think the same about each other never to their face they
can't stand the sight of each other or themselves
They were all friends once best friends until they lost their syndicate lotto winning
ticket suspicious that one of them might have had the winning ticket who nobody
knows so they grudgingly watch each other
For tell-tale signs all ten of them were given each a white envelop
With the lotto ticket in one of them after they had shuffled them up
When opened no lotto ticket found in any of them they accused each other of
deception
Five years have passed no ticket found the truth is one ticket won and the winnings
claimed by Mr Nobody or Some Body!

Face in a Crowd

I passed a face that looked like a face
From the past in the crowd stood out
A half turned glance a curious thought
In the morning rush
While flowing with the mass
Over the half penny bridge we go
Brollies trolleys boots and shoes
Each step like a drum beat sound
My eyes fix on a red feathered hat
Who is this follow I cannot remember
Closer look might remember
Too late the red hat has disappeared
And the face that housed it
Why waste time
Boots shoes and all are moving on
Can't move back with the mass moving forward
They are all with their partners their mobile phones except me
I lost the face from the past with the red feathered hat
Who could it have been who knows only the feathered hat on the head would know
the face.

Faces Remembered

Remember the faces, the peppermint smells
The bridge near the water pop mill
The fairground retreat
Where we gathered to meet
Our friends so dear to us all
The candy floss seat
Our coconut treat
The fun at the penny ball stand
The lemonade train
Our songs filled the air
With merriment laughter and fun
The horse ride delight on the merry go round
Cooled the warm summer breeze with its air
Near the band stand we danced
With the band in full flight
Sweet memories always recalled
Our parting farewells
Where we gathered to meet
Have faded away with the years
No longer the field with its fairground retreat
Or the band or the merry go round
Gone are those days
Only memories remain
And peppermint smells in the rain.

Fagan's About

Watch your pocket's Fagan's is about
In and out while you are still picking your green bogey nose
Gone without a good morning nod
Back around again before you could cough or sneeze which makes sense to Fagan
You could not see or hear him no one has ever seen him he likes it that way
As he likes to pick a pocket or two especially when the topic is about him
While you're on your cell phone he will leave you bewitched bothered and
bewildered distraught wondering where you left your car keys and your wallet
thinking you left them in your other coat that's what Fagan likes hear
And on he goes to the next nose picker who said it could never happen to him
That's the type of challenge Fagan likes to hear
So watch out Fagan's about no his already gone with the nose picker's wallet.

Fast Cook

There was a fast cook from Ballyagran who was fond of burning her pan
From breadcrumbs to puddings or bacon and chips
She knew she had to be fast
The puddings would jump with the shock of the fat
That boiled to melt metal and steel
Not that she cared this modern fast cook
When she turned her cooker to full.

Fellow Traveller

Do I share a simple thought with my fellow traveller,
Or hold back not to burden my quite companion,
Why should I remain silent when my mind is full of talk,
And my ears hear only footsteps on this silent journeys path,
No reason given to explain my demise or to speak out of turn,
Or laugh loudly without been heard,
Ungracious yes to my fellow journeyman,
Who respects my company and values my presents,
Yet whose very silence challenges my innermost thoughts,
And my reason to understand why I struggle with silence,
And why my companion is comfortable and familiar with silence,
I wonder what his thoughts are as we journeys on,
Maybe he meditates on the sounds he hears around him,
For me they would be a distraction to disrupt my thinking,
Yet without noticing my washing machine head has slowed down,
As I continued my journey along the road with my fellow traveller,
Who values my company and now I value his silences.

Field Of Dreams

Field of dreams bright colour shades
Harbour deep soft thoughts with landscapes painted without paint framed with
daisy chains
Those long summer days woven moments recalled locked in childhood memories
and worn out number games
Where summer shades and dancing thoughts met rainbow ends that have no ends
Over endless laugher talk and fun in our fields of dreams moments pass and friends
depart
Soon the winter covers our field of dreams shadows remain on moon lit nights
Who could imagine as years pass us by never to return those long summer days
And where have we wondered how far have we gone with our dreams and memories
and our field of dreams.

Find the Goose

Find the goose
Before the fox
The goose is loose
The fox is near and the goose for himself would be a treat
The ferret is also around and about also on the lookout for a loose goose
Farm boy Finch has found the wondering goose is now safely back in the chicken pen
The fox and the ferret are not happy their takeaway breakfast is found not lost.

Fourteen Not Seven

A family of seven lived with their shadows
Far in a woodland retreat where the sun light moonlight
Brings their shadows to life and fourteen not seven they became
They play dance talk together fun is had by all
When the clouds roll in it's time for a rest and seven not fourteen they become
Breakfast dinner or tea there is always a place at the table for their invisible
Family where conversion and cross sharing is eagerly shared
And when the clouds are gone and the sky is clear the moonlight sunlight returns
and out to play again and fourteen they become again.

Freddy the Fly

Freddy the fly is about where has he come from where has he been
You may well ask or guess when he lands on your bread and jam or your buttered
buns
Just passing through that's Freddy always ready to gate crash through your open
front door when he rings your bell
You can't see him or hear him he likes that way
He is patient waits for the bread and jam to arrive and the buttered buns
Freddy is never alone his friends are about ready for a dive bombing raid always
led by Freddy which sends the house people in to a uncontrollable frantic furious
waking the table with anything they can lay their hands or even Dads daily news
paper
To late Freddy and his friends are gone had their fell of sticky jam and buttered buns
And on to the next unsuspecting house Freddy and his friends are never homeless.

Free Man

Don't listen to the wayward man
Keep your penny in your hat by the side of your sack
And listen to the sound when the north wind blows through the holes in your shoes
it's a room with a view it could happen to you when you're singing the blues
Don't walk by where you walked before the road is long its short when you walk it
don't look back it might catch you up
Remember your hat a penny a mile its cold its warm seasons change
And you wayward man a free man with your penny in your hat a song to sing on the
open road of life's bends and twists road blocks endearing possibilities and many a
hill to climb to look over and view your country home

Don't listen to the wayward man keep your penny in your hat by the side of your
sack he may pass you by with nod or a smile on the road somewhere over the
rainbow of life's journeys end.

Gas Light Sally

Gas light Sally could tell a tale or two without looking at you
Or looking at who while cleaning her half broken glasses
To see who is to see or not to see
Sally always watches people passing by under the moon light not the gas light
She could tell a tale or two who cares what Sally sees or doesn't see
Sally is ghost after all she was a gas lighter until the gas lamp fell on her head
That was the end of poor Sally not so she's still around and about keeping watch
even with all the gas laps gone
And she is still the gas light Queen while cleaning her ghost like glasses
And watching you as you passing her by.

Glasses in the Rain

Come gather your thoughts near the old mill house
And sit on the bench near the river
With nothing to see
And nothing to hear
When the mind is distracted by trouble
And solutions untold are passing you by
In a hurry that makes no sense
Stop and make up, don't be a fool
When it comes to the push be ready
Go back inside the old mill house
And welcome yourself back home
You're home alone without your phone
And your glasses you left in the rain
Old memories are good when clouds cover the sun
And your mind sweeps along with the river
It's over and done there nothing to see or hear when the wondering mind imagines
whose calling
It's only a shadow on your kitchen wall that's always around when it's raining
When you are home alone on your own without your phone or your glasses in the
rain.

Goodbye Old Joe Bones

Goodbye old Joe Bones
Dead yes gone
Never coming back
Last seen with his pram and flag
Wearing his brown red feathered hat
Fell off the bridge with his pram and bones
Washed away down the river flow
Never again seen or heard
Only the old crow on the bridge with a brown red feathered hat
Last to have seen old Joe Bones hanging on to his pram of bones
Whose bones who knows the butcher shop bones said the old crow on the bridge
with the red feathered hat
Goodbye old Joe with your pram of bones
Said the old crow on the bridge as he lifted his hat
And flew down the river with a happy crows squawk.

Harry the Fish

Harry the fish has arrived for tea its fish again said Harry
To his cat and dog named Ready and Steady
I eat fish when I am hungry I eat fish when I am not hungry said Harry and Ready
and Steady agreed as they can eat fish any time
Harry lives with his Father fisherman Sam and his Mother fish seller Pam
Whose family have always lived on fish without a hitch
The locals call them the fish cake family because they always smell of fish
All the town folk are fish cakes themselves as they to live on fish
Harry celebrated his twenty first birthday party
At the Old Fishnet Inn all the town folk were there plus Ready and Steady
For a great fish cake party of singing dancing fun for all and Harry sang his favourite
rendition of I love my fish in the morning I love my in the evening I love my fish
anytime and they all clapped and cheered and sang Harry's happy birthday song
then they all joined in to do two step fish cake dance
And the town folk presented Harry with a very special birthday cake in the shape of
a fish with twenty one fish like candles
And Harry the fish as he is better known thanked all for a wonderful twenty first
birthday party celebration and they all sang and danced the night away to the towns
favourite band the rocking fish cakes.

Henry the House Mouse

Henry the house mouse
Sleeps in a cupboard
When his not hungry
That's not often
Not very often
He's a hungry little mouse
Who likes to eat and have some fun
When the house people and their cat are fast asleep up stairs
His not alone his friends are around to keep watch eat and have some fun too
When the house people and their cat are awake
Henry returns to hide and sleep in his cupboard
While his friends are asleep in their mouse holes
Until the house people and their cat are asleep again in dream land
And Henry and his friends meet again in search of any food left over by the house
people and their sleeping cat
Henry and his friends enjoyed their stay until a new cat arrived a mouse eating cat
who refused to share his house with any mice
Including the sleeping cat upstairs all had to go
Henry and his friends found a new home while the sleeping cat is now asleep in the
cat's home.

Hopping Lady

You never stop
Hop Hop Hopping
There you go close to my heart
Pop Pop Popping
Merry go round you make me laugh
Yes Yes Yes
Close to my heart
Never stop missing you
Love Love Love
You're close to my heart never stop missing you
Kiss Kiss Kiss
You talk too much you hop to much
On the bus train shop and in the rain
Hop Hop Hopping
There you go you lost your shoes you lost your coat
Pop Pop Popping
I love you now I love you then
With your hands on your hips
Kiss Kiss Kiss
Love Love Love you make me laugh
When you go Shout Shout Shout
Hold me tight don't let go
It's all in your day
Here we go again you make me dance
Hop Hop Hopping
Pop Pop Popping
Kiss Kiss Kissing
Where did you come from
Over the back road beyond the hills
That's not far when you go Hop Hop Hopping
Smile Smile Smiling
Kiss kiss kissing
Hop Hop Hopping
Smile Smile Smiling
Wave Wave Wave
Goodbye and we are out of sight

In the Dog House

Jim the dog is in the kennel
Poor Jim
And Pinch the dog is asleep in the house
On Jim's comfortable chair
While Jim is in Pinches kennel
With his six pack for comfort
Why is poor Jim in the kennel?
His good wife
Not that Jim thinks so
Kicked him out because of his drinking behaviour
That's why Jim the dog is in the doghouse
And Pinch is asleep in Jim's chair
Not that he's complaining
And neither is Jim
After drinking 8 cans of the best
Only his good wife is not happy
Because Pinch and Jim are happy
Poor Jim in the dog house
Is feeling no pain.

Jack's Lament

Come back come back with my bread and cheese sandwiches
Cried careless Jack to the duck who had stolen his lunch
What can I do what can I say to a duck who can swim and fly
The duck agreed Jack is right as he ate his bread and cheese sandwiches
Not that he cared for poor Jacks demise for an opportunity taken by a cleaver duck
Jack went home cried a little and made more bread and cheese sandwiches
Not for the duck only Jack who will shout no more
Come back come back with my bread and cheese sandwiches.

Joe the Hat Is Lost

Joe the hat is lost disappeared without a trace with his be loveable dog one eye Patch
Ten years have passed and no sign of the Hat or Patch
To where have they gone who could care less after all those years
Not so his good lady and her five children two stay cats a hen a duck and a useless
rabbit
She has a new life a new man who has no interest in dog's cat's hen's ducks or a
useless rabbits
She is kind of happy hoping the Hat or Patch don't return as there is a new man
around the house who is nervous as he himself disappeared from his family ten years
ago always looking out the window just in case they might find him
What keeps them really nervous the children keep dreaming that the
Hat and Patch are on the way back so the children's two stray cats the hen duck and
the useless rabbit are happy that way
Which keeps the good lady and her not so new man around the house on their toes.

Key for the Door for the Dog

Outside, inside, looking out
Notice
Dog is out somewhere
My garden no
Someone's garden
Whose garden
His garden, trouble brewing
Two spoons in my tea make light of it
Act deaf
In the head like them

Outside inside looking out
The dog is always out
Dog's choice
My fault they imagine
No the dogs fault he's out not me
Wish he was out of my mind and them

Outside, inside looking out
He's back again wagging his tail behind him
What would he expect from them not the dog
Here they come, himself with his prize rose in his hand
Wish I was somewhere else

Outside inside looking out
Blame who Blame me. Blame the dog.
He was out not me
Who let him out
Himself he's got a key
Water for the rose
There's always next year shouted someone
Or the year after shouted the dog
Oh dear don't say it's only a rose
That will grow again next year
Listen to himself and his rose whose talking
And we are all outside, inside, looking out
His shouting she's crying
We are half outside inside looking out don't speak
show concern without moving your lips
While the dog is inside looking out wagging his tail

finishing off another bowel of fresh creamy milk for his breakfast.

King Tim Tack

Many centuries long ago, there lived a very unusual king who was loved and adored by his subjects, his kingdom lay in a valley surrounded by mountains and hills. His hobby was making shoes and boots for his subjects also teaching his subjects how to make boots and shoes for themselves. The terrain of his kingdom was gravel and sharp stones that cut his peoples feet so with his shoes and boots his people were able to go about their business without injuring their feet. It was a very peaceful time in this extraordinary kingdom until an ambitious king in an adjoining kingdom was expanding his territory he had ruthlessly taken over many other kingdoms and the last one on the list was Tim Tacks kingdom so he primed and prepared his army to take over and occupy Tim Tacks kingdom although Tim Tack had no weapons or army to match this aggressive king only one defence they had was their very sharp gravel stones which the aggressive king knew nothing about. After ten days of marching towards Tim Tacks castle the aggressive king and his army's inferior footwear began to wear out as well as the kings footwear so the last five days before they reached Tim tacks castle his army were suffering and crying their eyes out with the pain of their feet against the rugged sharp stones that tore their feet to shreds. When the two kings met Tim Tack looked at the opposing kings feet and saw the extent of the injury and the king ordered the servants to wash and bandage the opposing kings feet and the king ordered his subjects to show kindness and care to the army and wash their feet and cream to stop them crying when the opposing kings feet were almost
healed Tim Tack made a pair of boots for the king and the subjects made pairs of boots for the army. The opposing king was astonished
by the kindness and care of the king Tim Tack that he signed a decree that he would not oppose king Tim Tack again and make his way back to his own kingdom and withdraw from all the other kingdoms he had occupied and never to invade Tim Tacks kingdom or any other kingdom so Tim Tacks kingdom continued to live in peace as they always have done.

Lady in a Bottle

In a bottle stands a lady near the town of Ballincrea,
How she got there ask the sailor who brought her from the sea,
In a bottle he will tell you stood a lady small and fair,
So the sailor took the bottle to his home in Ballincrea,
If you ask him where the house is and the lady small and fair,
He will tell you in a bottle near the town of Ballincrea.

Lamplighter Dan

Lamplighter Dan lived with his wife named Pam
Walking in the forest one night together Dan's lamp went out in the blink of an eye
and a cough when Pam's teeth flew out
Oh dear oh dear what can we do when everything around us is black
Never mind your lamp cried Pam my gums are lost without my teeth
Worry or not said lamplighter Dan to his wife named Pam your toothless gums can
get used to no teeth like my head when my hair feel out
What can we do is there any way out of this forest and back to our home cried Pam
without my teeth and your hairless head
Let us sit and wait under this old oak tree until the morning comes and together we
will find our way home smiled lamplighter Dan to himself as they both feel asleep
under the oak
Next morning they woke and found themselves back in their beds and found they
were only dreaming Pam's teeth was back in her gums and Dan's hair was back on his
head what amazed them both they had the same dream
And lamplighter Dan found his night time lamp with no oil had gone out the only
part of their dream that was real
Lamplighter Dan and his wife named Pam shared the same dream the next night
this time Dan's lamp never went out or Pam's teeth never fell out and Dan's hair
remained on his head.

Len the Shadow

Sam the man lost his shadow one day,
On the way down gum tree lane,
His shadow named Len,
Was shy and reserved,
Too proud to speak or interrupt when Sam was talking fast,
Waiting his turn to speak,
He spoke faster than Sam,
Both continued down gum tree lane,
Talking and cross talking,
Until they joined together,
When the light of the sun was no more,
And Sam and Len could talk no more.

Lime Bucket and Brush

The old lime washed walls
Repainted many times over
Family annual tradition
Brush and bucket handed down
To the next generation to continue
To cover up the turf stained smoke filled walls
And leave their mark on the family tree
And clean the old rose picture on the wall
Nannies favourite
In the corner stands grandpas old blue rocking chair
We still imagine him sitting there
With his pipe in his mouth
In his hand a mug of black tea
Yet departed many years
Now I'm the grandpa sitting in the blue rocking chair
Without a pipe or mug of black tea in hand
Only a can in both hands cheers.

Locked Down Charlie

Locked down Charlie is always lock in or locked out or thrown out
He likes it that way not so much the bruises and bumps on his out of shaped head
and body it's his wild life style
He joined the lock down club and found he could fit in or out
Whichever way he was thrown through the door and back again
He found the club unfriendly that's part of their success which helps him to fit in or
out
Now a proud member of the locked down club which helps him practice soft
landings not on his head or on his bones
Less hospital visits are welcome for Charlie the hospital agrees as they are running
out of Plaster of Paris for treating Charlie's broken bones.

London Club

Farrington Charlie
London club
King of fashion
Side show maker
Lost his club
To a lady named Vera the Lip
Who sold it and went to live in Cairo
Without Farrington Charlie
Vera the Lip never came back and died without a penny
Farrington Charlie did come back
From where he could not say
He bought back his club
His London club
And called it The Queen Vera the Lip Of Cairo.

Long Time Moving Son

Long time moving son, there's knocking on my door
Where's my shoes Where's my socks there's knocking at the door
The light went out some time ago there's knocking at the door
I'm moving on to dreams gone by
There's knocking at the door
Someone's outside having fun
Alone inside I'm here
I'm out of touch the worlds gone by
There's knocking at my door
My mirror cracked there's three of us looking back at me
I'm so confused I 'm not all there who's knocking at my door
I would sing a song if I knew the words
There's knocking at my door
My coat and hat are somewhere else my socks have found my feet
I've had my breakfast tea and biscuits there's knocking on my door
Open my door it's only my cat who's knocking on my door.

Lost Dog

Have you seen John Majors dog, not sense he lost him in the park ten years ago
Colour Red, Blue at night when the moon shines bright
Responds to the name Bosco John lost when he went to look for his plastic bone
Poor John Majors Red Setter his pride and joy disappeared with or without his
plastic bone and never came back, ten years to the day, seems like yesterday
John Major looked with some regret for Bosco John, now he has another Red Setter
called Brexit John who has a phone not a bone, and lost maybe not as his on his
masters Brexit lead with his plastic phone not his bone.

Lost in a Dream

The night seems fine when the lights go out
And tired heads are asleep
Time to roll over and back again
Start all over again another day
With a smile or a cry for help
Sound of music singing people at play
Some at work some not at work
Some could not care less they are not up yet
And where have all the other people gone
Lost disappeared maybe somewhere over the rainbow
Colours bright good times are here for some not all
Waste of time follow the pack join in where you can if you can or carry the can
It's all a joke loose talk means nothing who's over the hill who's back again
Find yourself hiking around and around the apple tree
Join the crowed fall in not the apples
And wake the others up it's all a dream anyway.

Man and Bike at the Town Gate

Who is the man in red with the red painted bike
A stranger at the town gate rearranging his red feathered hat
Red checked buttons on his red camel coat trousers to match
Not a journey man or a man of the open road
The town agree as they passed him by with a welcome nod or two
Acknowledged by the stranger as he deep's his red feathered hat with a red
face smile
The town Mayor who had been asked by the nosy and inquisitive town folk to
approach the stranger the man in red and red bike to match and welcome him
officially to the town who himself was curious about the unusual man in red bike to
match
the stranger however beckoned the town folk to come near and spoke not a word
with a smile he touched his hat and he became a man of green and bike to match he
touched his hat again and he became a man of blue and bike to match the town folk
where amazed as he changed colour after colour and bike to match then suddenly he
disappeared from there sight gone and never returned
The mystery remains many town folk have heard a bicycle bell ringing during the
night time coming from the town gate just before the gate clock strikes two.

Melonacther Road

It was there she did pass me no need to ask her,
Where she was after on the road to Melonacther,

She came by that road Seven times did I pass her
Nor did I ask her where she was after,
On the road to Melonacther,

Many times ever after I hurried to pass her
But never to find her on the road to Melonacther,

I looked ever after to find her to ask her,
Yet never to pass her if only to ask her,
Where she was after On the road to Melonacther.

Millers Farmyard Wall

The barking dogs on Millers farmyard wall
Woke the blue brown chicken
For her early morning lay
At nine past nine
Farmyard time
By Millers farmyard clock
That never stopped
Since the blue brown chicken came
To wake the dogs
The barking dogs at Millers farmyard wall

Millie the Tap Dancer

Millie is tap dancer her friend is a bouncer who cannot dance.
But can bounce heads over and around to the beat of Millie's tap dancing skill
Which suits Millie with heads bouncing on wooden floors which gives an unusual beat
The Biscuit boys they like to call themselves arrive not for dancing trouble is there night out which gives the bouncer his favourite heads to throw and bounce on wooded floors which suits the Biscuit boys they like it that way
Giving them a sense of belonging as Millie's friend the bouncer calls them wooden heads for wooded floors and Millie enjoys herself with her tap dancing Routine giving the Biscuit boys heads a good make over with her favourite tap dance number called heads for taps the Biscuit boys declare another good night out at the dance club as they realize that was only part one of their night out as the blue lights are waiting outside for the Biscuit boys to practice their drumming skill on wooden heads as they also like to call them with their new state of the art truncheons.
Millie the tap dancer and her friend the bouncer also agree the tap dancing club the best night ever the Biscuit boys however agreed after their heads shapes returned to normal although they agreed they looked better after their great tap dance night out looking forward to another great night out at tap dancing club once the rest of the plaster comers off the rest of their bodies
Millie the tap dancer and her friend the bouncer have sent the Biscuit boys a get well card we miss you looking forward to you coming back which touched the hearts not their sore heads of the Biscuit boys.
The blue lights not to be left out also sent their get well cards as we miss you and look forward to another night of blue light truncheon drumming to the beat off Millie's head tapping blues.

Mirror Thoughts

Weep quietly to yourself young man
Turn your face away from those mirror thoughts
Rush towards those northern lights
Where yesterday's years have been forgotten
Memories, brick walls, slabs and wire cutters
Without exception
Years gone by
Blink open a new age
Old age
Weep quietly old man while the onlookers pass you by.

Misty Blue Shoes

The dancing queen
Of the Mississippi tar boat song
Who commands great enthusiastic applause
With her rendition of the river boat blues
Encore after encore followed
Until she called all to come and join the dance
The band played and the people jived and swayed to the beat of the river boat blues
With fish a-jumping
The frogs are croaking
And the trees are swaying
And the river boat moving
Down the old Mississippi river
And Misty blue shoes still dancing in the moonlight
And the wheels are turning
And the smoke from the funnels pouring out gently, upward
As if enjoying the music
And Misty blue shoes continues to sing again
Her rendition of the river boat blues.

Moments

Moments gone moments lost
A moment in time
Before and after the last moment
Thinking about nothing for a moment
Funny moments
Quiet moments
Sad moments, departing moments
Friendly moments
Goodbye moments
Moments and moments
Moments without a break
Divert your thoughts to the last moment
Find which moment suits you the best
Then run, run, run and find a quiet moment to rest your mind
Or you may find your last moments have all gone by without you
Moments too long moments too short moments too remember moments to forget
and a moment too late when you fade away too dark brown grey.

Moody Blues

Moody Blues you left me low,
Remember when you waved goodbye,
In the wind and the rain without a word just faded out of sight,
You moved away no reason given only memories linger
Your painted picture on the wall captured those still quite moments spent together
All seems empty now without you by my side
Your words of comfort soon where lost
Faded in some dark corner of my mind
You said you had to leave to find your journeys end
That was just a year ago
I look out along the long road in the distance I imagine I still see you there
And where are you now where have you gone
Out of sight to some distance place to find your journey's end
And all I have is your painted picture on my wall
Where memories still linger till I find my own journey's end.

Moon Shadow

The dance was over the crowd had gone
All quiet
The moon shadow through the smoke stained skylight
With some movement on the polished dance floor
And there stood I a dreamer of sorts
Thinking to myself
As the moon shadow spread its carpet lights all around me
Maybe a step or two
With my moon shadow
Out of tune out of step
And that's okay
It's the moon dance with my shadow on the floor.

Moonlight Shadows

Moonlight shadows filter in and out of moving tree branches
Making many interesting shapes
On old Joe the Pipes lime washed woodland cottage
Never alone thought old Joe
Sat on his moss covered wooden bench
Smoking his Pipe
He made from the bark of his beloved oak tree
And the dry leaves gathered
And rolled to make his homemade tobacco
Yet he could sit for many hours
Looking at something and talking to those strange shadow shapes
Did they answer back
Who knows only old Joe the Pipe
And the shadows on his lime washed walls.

Moonlight Shine

We danced without a moonlight shine
In the garden of our dreams
We looked we thought for a little while
How could it be so real
Yet the music played
 Songs were sung
And smiles and laughter too
Filled the air with heartfelt words of joy
And all that time the band played on
And round and round we danced
Until the time to wake and share those dreams that seemed so long ago.

Music Man

He who stood
Without some notice
Humming away to himself
While foot tapping on the hard wooded floor
A red captains hat
To match his blue brown trousers
Yellow socks
Pink suede shoes
Conducting to himself
With his blue grey gloves
If only his Nan could see him now
Departed with a free ticket to her eternal home
Which made sense to him
She would have been proud of him
The only one who appreciated his music
Now only his cat and dog are his audience
That's ok he smiled
It's not about numbers it's the music that counts
Said the cat and the dog
And the music man agreed.

My Rose Of Old Kentucky Town

I smiled and said goodbye my love
My rose of old Kentucky town
The sun was shining all around
The day my love said goodbye
She looked and turned her head away
I knew she said goodbye
Kentucky town I remember leaving that summer's day
Without my rose I'm on the road again
And when I see the sign post
Leading me far away
From my rose my only rose of old Kentucky town.

Name On the Board

Gather your thoughts
Leave nothing behind
Remember you're the first
The last in the queue
Stand by and get ready
Ready with teddy
With your name on the board
Where the silent and noisy rush by in a hurry

Goodbye to the neighbours
Who hide behind curtains
Wave to the postman
The milkman has gone
Walk slow don't hurry
Make way for your story
With your name on the board
Where the silent and noisy rush by in a hurry

Don't look at your face
It's beginning to rain
The night time has gone
The morning has found your name on the board
Where the silent and noisy rush by in a hurry

Your face is the face
The last of the year
Good laughter and fun
We were once in the sun
Good morning has come
With your name on the board
Where the silent and noisy rush by in a hurry

The night time has found
The morning no fun
Your tea has gone cold
Your hairs in a mess
Don't look at the news
Has yesterday gone?
With your Name on the board
Where the silent and noisy rush by in a hurry.

Needless Joe

Needless Joe walked a mile back
With his punctured bike in toe
Unable to think just kept kicking his bike
And blaming it for his demise
On missing out on the pedal day rally
Has only himself to blame
To leave without a puncture outfit
Needless Joe stop kicking your bike and breaking the spokes on your wheels
Or stop and give your bike to the scrap man like you always do
Who will understand with a comforting smile
Which makes no sense to needless Joe only his buckled bike
Who is glad to retire to the scrap yard to avoid any more frustrated kicking
Goodbye Needless Joe said the smiling scrap man look forward
To seeing you again next year when you forget your puncture outfit once again
Needless Joe.

Nosey Nancy

Nosey Nancy had a friend who also liked been nosey,
in other people's business, busy body's nosey parkers,
Yes they could not mind their own business
Or any ones business, especially their friends if they had any,
With their prying eyes and hearing aids
They like to listen into what their neighbours have to say specially when their
neighbours can't see them
Good news bad news no problem to them,
As long as it was more bad than good,
To exaggerate is their business,
More to talk about and more to add to,
Nancy and her friend never fall out even when they talk about each other's business,
over cup of coffee and a biscuit to share,
Gossip they enjoy together when they feel a bit low,
Which cheers them up.

Old Dan the Joe

The red painted chair
In the middle of a large painted room without a view
Where no one has lived since old Dan the Joe finished his time on earth
Unable to take his beloved tins of paint
Or his treasured paintbrushes with him
Had no time to say goodbye
Or change the colour of his only chair from yellow to red
Yet someone or somebody has
Mr nobody shouted a friend with a red painted can
Or his woman with her rose coloured hair
Who knows maybe old Dan the Joe is back from the dead
Or the woman with the rose coloured hair.
Or himself with his red painted can
Or has Old Dan the Joe been and gone from the room without a view.

Old Jack the Bike

Do not disturb old jack while he's cleaning his bike
For the annual pedal man's bike race
Around the old oak tree
And back to the blue Cross Garage to finish
Eagerly awaited this year's pedal man's bike race
By all who will take part
Two wheeled bicycles only
Not scooters or wheelchairs
One winner only a great prize
A pair of reconditioned tyres for his or her bike
The rest of the field, a packet of puncture outfits
Old jack always finishes last
Not that he's bothered
Its taking part is what's important
And free beer for all the pedal men at the Old Bike Inn
And they all agree that's what's really important
Said Old Jack the Bike.

Old Joe Bones Has Gone

The old mill house is empty now
Now covered in moss and rot
Every broken window pane a story once was told
And he that lived and died within could never find a wife
He travelled far he travelled wide no promise ever made
And back again to a hermit's life
And all that was left was his own dry bones found many years after
A note left said he loved life but found no wife
Signed Old Joe Bones has gone.

Old Sawdust Mill

Billy Mcthe park bench scare crow
Sits with a half sarcastic smile with a wave to his friend
Jimmy Mcthe new owner of the old derelict sawdust mill
Best friends true journey men of the open road
Not any more sense Jimmy Mcpulled a piece of paper out of Billy Macs park bench
waste paper basket which happened to be the last will and testament of the previous
owner of the old sawdust mill whoever finds this paper is the new owner of the old
mill
Poor Billy Mclost out fell asleep before he could check his waste paper basket
While Jimmy Mcchecked it instead and inherited the old sawdust mill
But Jimmy Mcsoon lost interest in the old mill he missed the open road he resumed
his friendship with Billy Mcscare crow and agreed to share the old sawdust mill with
him so they could use it for their winter shelter
So the two best friends are back on the open road again.

Olive for Tea

Is it true it's only Olive that came for tea
May I say without a question or two
Why Olive not Olive
Or Olive who came to tea
On a sunset good afternoon
It's only Olive dear Olive
Sweet Olive, smiling Olive, laughing Olive
Crying Olive
Why did she come for tea
Who invited her
Herself it's her home after all
Who invited you
Olive did, sweet caring Olive
And what's your name Olive
I am Olive for tea.

One Night Stop in Ballyagran

One night stop in Ballyagran
No buses trains or taximen
Phoned my Mom said hello
Lost without my plastic phone
Cried into my pint of draught
Found it funny when I had no money
Played my harp everybody danced
Combed hair said ok
Walked into the cool night air
Ballyagran you're a happy man
A good time son of a wayward man
Castletown on road I came
Made some money when I sold some honey
Passing through to Colman's well
And on to dance in Charleville
Say hello to the girl I met the table dancer with the nut brown hair
Ask her Dad without delay if she would marry in the month of May
So ill sing my song along the way
One night stop in Ballyagran no buses trains or taxi men.

Out of Sight

Reflective colour shapes you are,
Reflective colour shapes,
A moment lost,
A moment gone,
To dwell upon your sight,
How beautiful your shape stood out in the window of my heart,
To soon recall your loving smile, your soft brown eyes and all,
And yet a dream a glance a pass,
In the window of my heart.

We failed to know the time was right,
How could we not be sure,
The difference between us then,
Remains in some years night,
Easy company shared with care,
Unspoken words so clear,
Your parting sight your half turned glance moved my eyes to tears,
We failed to know the time was right,
As we faded out of sight.

Peter Flea

Peter flea the flea bite king,
Can hop from town to town,
And in each house he loves to play come catch me if you can,
For if you can't he will catch you first and play his flea bite game,
So jump away you young and old and don't let Peter flea,
For if you don't his friends will play the flea bite game instead.

Picture Photo

Long term friend finds a picture
In a picture of his friend
Finds his mother and his brother
In the picture of his friend
Shows his aunty and his uncle
The picture of his friend
His aunty shows his uncle
His brother in the picture of his friend
His brother finds his long lost sister
In the picture of his friend
His mother's aunty finds her aunty in the picture of his friend
His father thinks he's found his cousin in the picture of his friend
They all could see they found each other
In the picture of his friend
And his friend found himself in the picture of his friend.

Pie Man Sam

Pie man Sam is back with a new pie on his way to the pie man's fair
Proud pie man Sam hopes to win again the top pie prize as he lives and breathes
walks talks pies even dreams about pies
Sam's family are all pie makers as he comes from a long line of pie makers and is
related to the first great pie taster Simple Simon who met the first great pie man on
the way to the pie man's fair
Pie man Sam knows history is on his side and hopes to win again
Not so with the other competitors who believe there pies are better than Sam's and
should win on merit but feel the pie judges always favours Sam pies owning to his
ancestral family line of pie makers and related to the first great pie taster Simple
Simon commercially it makes sense to Sam for he knows he draws the crowds to the
fair with his ancestral family background and all the other competitors need not
complain as they benefit from the extra crowd as they sell more pies at the fair than
all the year round
Pie man Sam wins again not surprising and a new name for the fair Simple Simon
pie man's fair

Plastic Phone Anxiety

Panic stations frantic search upside down unable to think
Fear in contact with my mind while texting twittering me unable to sit stand or lie
down
The loss of my cell phone is beyond my comprehension unable to contact the
outside world friend's family anyone only my head is in contact with my nerviest
system the search goes on and on
Where is my councillor when I need someone to talk to
one hour gone like a life time
An earthquake has hit my dwelling place I need help I'm finished lost abandoned oh
dear my fingers are sending me texts on my table top
My phone has been kidnapped by Mr know body or somebody
Lay the blame where you can I cannot go on scratching my head my brain is in
over drive how can anyone survive without their plastic cell impossible to cope and
remain sane without a visit to ones local GP
Part of myself is closed down shut off any logical understanding or common sense
has gone through the window of my mind's eye view
A day time nightmare while awake
My girlfriend said I have to choose between my phone or her
I said I love my mobile phone threes a crowd she said closed door and never came
back my phone has left me It's not coming back
Without my phone I feel homeless abandoned alone heartbroken
Helpless a leaper castaway no friends my doctor said this to shall pass he was right
crisis over cell phone found in my cats basket who was using It to order more milk.

Ploughman Sidney

Ploughman Sidney's beloved horse Wilberforce has died
Fourteen long years an all weather plough horse hail rain wind or snow
A true loyal worker helping Sidney keeping the ridges straight
Poor Sidney knew that Wilberforce would be the last plough shire horse
The end of an era a true family tradition going back to Sidney's great grandfather's
time
Yet Sidney is happy again the first of a new family tradition with his new red tractor
named Wilberforce the second
Sidney's farming friends said it was about time he had a tractor twenty years late not
that it bothered Sidney better late than never and Wilberforce the tractor agrees.

Poor Benny

Benny the slug
Lives in an old mug
By the side of an old compost heap
With plenty of food to share with none
He is as happy as a slug in mud
Yet with a look of despair
No friend to play
Or a cabbage patch to call his own
Only a slow snail crawl around his heap
Then back to his mug to sleep
Poor Benny the slug is asleep.

Poor Man at the Door

Poor man at the door he sat without a pipe
Or a glass of something
Stronger than water
Unable to train at present
Due to a snuff fit of uncontrollable sneezing
Dislodging his brown denchers
And snuffbox hearing aids
When they flew from his person with such gusty
Disappearing out of sight somewhere over the rainbow
And wondering to himself with some trepidation
If he would be able to attend the annual snuff head nose convention
As he is late removing the brown clinkers from his brown stained nose
And would be unable to compete in his favourite snuff head sneezing challenge
Ten sneezes per minute to win ten boxes of best brown snuff.

Rag Man Black Bat

Never in a hurry
Careful collector of worn out clothes
Eagle eyed observer
Spots a bargain from a distance
Well known to all
Liked by all
This jolly rag man Black Bat
Sings his rendition of any old rags
With his rusty old pram and its squeaky wheels
Works in all weathers
It's his job
Where he lives where he goes nobody knows

Rag man Black Bat is dead
Found buried amongst his rags
In his hut filled with bag after bag of rags
Poor Black Bat
Gone without his beloved rags
Which will be cleared In skip after skip
And ferried to the local council tip incinerator goodbye Black Bat.

Rambling Round the Old Road

I rambled round the old road
Those many years ago
Where I first met my true love
And friends and neighbours too
When I said I would be leaving
To lands across the sea
And my love asked me if I would return again
I promised her I would and she will be my bride
And now I have returned and many years have passed
A stranger now in my land
And strangers they are too
My love has gone neighbours too
To lands far away
And promises I made were lost in foreign lands
And many more like me whose dreams have passed away
Never again to return for they too have passed away.

Rock Star Music Man

Burnt out music man
Sold out in the rain
Over the top
Under the weather
Yesterday's man
Critical comment
Reviews disappointing
Struggling rock star
Remembered, yes remembered
Your history said the twelve year old
Not another tour
What for? Music man
Slow down and retire
Play with your memories
Live in the past or face another day
History maker
Music maker
Not good news
Tears
This too shall pass
Like you music man
Don't call us call someone else
Said the twelve year old
As he picked his lollypop nose.

Sam and His Ham

A well known man
Who drank his drink from a can
He bought a pan
To cook his ham
He lived in a house without any doors
Windows without any glass
With a cat and a dog
And a mouse who came through the open front door
All together they help Sam eat his ham
Without burning his pan
Said the mouse who came through his open front door.

Show Me

Don't tell me show me
Said the pigeon in the loft
To the washing machine head
Who stood outside
And had a break from his snatcher friends
And the finger pointers
Who came late to have their usual rant
About something or nothing
That makes no sense
Only to the pigeon in the loft
And the washing machine head
Who found the washing powder box
In the snatcher's pockets.
And the squirrels with their nuts agreed.

Shutters Down

Broken rusty gadgets moving windows open shutters down,
Pressure out of sorts running past the winning post,
Empty sidewalks full of litter moved on by an angry breeze,
Signpost viewing out of sight near Scarecrow Corner around Gypsy Bend,
Well done to those who won a bun said someone somewhere having fun,
Open the door the wild cats moving over the feet of the footless shoes,
The bats are awake all over the place where the cardboard lady lays her head
Wait until the moon goes down to mend the broken rusty frame,
Gadgets moving windows open shutters down here comes the rain,
Start again and face the day where the beggar man plays his morning song, and the
bag lady leaves her cardboard box,
The wild cat returns with a mouse in his mouth who cares little for broken windows
or shutters down,
We won't delay we are on the move and back again to face the night-time movers
fixers sorters to mend without delay before the heavy rain comes down on the
Broken rusty gadgets moving widows open shutters down.

Sidney Drover Tight Rope Walker

Sidney Drover tight rope walker
Lost his balance thought he could fly
Met the floor coming up
Convinced in his head he could fly like a bird
Sidney Drover ex tight rope walker
Long time stay in bone mead hospital
Will never again walk the line
Or try to fly like a bird on his Zimmer frame
Sidney Drover last great tight rope walker
Remembered yes remembered
The day he tried to walk the line
Blindfolded with a bag of potatoes on his head
And down he came like a bird without wings
With the bag of potatoes on his head
Well done Sidney Drover your name is remembered on the tight rope walker's hall of
fame.

Someone's Daughter, Someone's Son

Someone's daughter, someone's son
Who is he? Who is she?
Where is she from? Where is he from?
Who joined who
Did she? Did he?
Whose life is her life? Whose life is his life?
She takes care of things
He takes care of himself
She looks after the children
He looks after himself
She takes the children to school
He takes the dog for a walk
She picks the children up from school
He picks a horse to win
She calls the children for their tea
He calls for another pint
She gets the children ready for bed
He gets ready for another pint
She tells the children a bedtime story
He tells his friends to get another round in
She falls asleep waiting for him
He's carried home not because he's got a bad leg
She's up next morning
He's upside down on the armchair
She calls the children for school
He calls for tea
She calls him a no good fool
He calls her a bitch
She calls him a loser
He calls her a big mouth all talk
She calls him a boozer
He calls her a foolish stupid person
She calls the children for school
He calls the dog for a walk
She takes the children to school
He takes the dog for a walk
She leaves him
He lives alone with his dog
Someone's daughter, someone's son
Someone's granddad, someone's grandma
Who is she? Who is he?

Someone's Son

The man in the corner
A shape without hope
Paper cup in hand
Cries out for a handout
Someone's son
Background history
Hopeless son unwanted
Wayward kid
Spoilt with violence and rejection
End not known
What day it could be
Still in yesterday
Half in tomorrow
Today makes no sense
When you're lost in the moonlight
On a cold frosty night
The man in the corner a shape unknown
Why worry it's not your fault
Mr Somebody
For you only noticed
A Nobody Mr. Somebody.

Sorry John

Sorry John lost out
In a game of cards he thought he could win
He lost his boots
He lost his wife
House and money
Quicker than he could sneeze or cough
He cried bitter tears on the way to the bank
And found all he had left was IOUs
Bootless socks
A goodbye note from his wife
And a thank you note from the winner
Who said he would be happy to play him again
When his winnings ran out
Funny or not a loser's demise
A man of the road he became
What happened to sorry john?
He found a new wife a job and a house
And he never again played cards where winner takes all
When he died
The description on his headstone read
Sorry John who lies here lived all his life feeling sorry for himself.

Stone Cutter Jack

Stone cutter Jack
Makes impressions of himself
Nobody else only himself
He lives in a house built of stone
For himself by himself
His house is full of Jacks
Like himself for himself
They sit at the table
Standing around
Upstairs downstairs
Every room Is full of Jacks
They are so like Jack
You would hardly notice the real Jack
Stone cutter Jack is never alone
By himself for himself
With all his Jacks.

Sweet Harvest Jane

Don't knock the door sweet harvest Jane
You're out and about when the full moon shines
You're shadow on my wall meets your shadow coming back
You're parting farewell to your picture on my wall
And in to the moon light you faded out sight
Your thoughts are not main when you rang my phone
Your lonesome song was out of tune
That was before the harvest moon
When the world seemed new not so now
You moved on when you shut the door
And your shadow on the wall has moved on to
All that is left is our lonesome blues
On harvest moon as seasons change.

Ted at the Door

A foot with a sock
And a shoe made of gold
Arrive without ringing the bell
Unusual comments remarked by some
Surprised with a snigger or a sneeze
The bell rang again
The door opened wide
The sock and the shoe said hello
The boy with his head said come on in
You're welcome without making a fuss
Mind the step and the painted door
Painted some ten years before the spider climbed out of his web
Said Ted
Whose ted they said
The spider said the head
The head lead them through to the room with a view
Where they gathered to wait for the glove
The glove appeared through a hole in the wall
And remarked without saying a word
They all agreed it made sense to them
So the glove and the shoe
Without question or doubt
Agreed to meet again
The head with the bell said it sounds good to them
And the glove found time to agree
And a song was sung of farewell goodbye
As the mouse ran under the floor
So the foot with the sock and the shoe made of gold
Departed without saying a word
For they knew they would meet their friends again
And Ted if it came to the push

Teddy Freddy's Party

Teddy Freddy joins the party
Jelly cakes and custard pies
Yellow greens and red balloons
Colours galore fun for all
Whose party? Everyone's.
Cried Cindy peg with laughter
Ourselves included friends to meet
Chat about nothing talk about something
Maybe dance a step or two
Remarked, Milly pear drop candy top
To her friend Ollie shoe polish bright shine
Interrupted by a hidden smile and a nod
Without embarrassment or comment
Views untold just fun, run, hide and seek
Enjoyment by all
More jelly cakes and custard pies
Eaten without concern
Thought Jenny Mc-hat
To her friend Mavis jelly bean butter cup
Carrot heads
Turnip tops
Cabbage leaves
With mushroom smiles
And party poppers
With their friends and carers
They danced the day away
And played their party games
Then thanked and said goodbye to each other
And they all joined teddy Freddy
As he played his last jelly bean dance
Without a compliment
On his straw string loot
And they all nodded with agreement
That the jelly cake custard pie party
Was the best ever.

The Annual Brown Duck Race

Brown duck race encounters small honour without price given,
Annual field event not advertised
By invitation only
Rules enforced
Brief clapping only
To those trained in the art
Shouting forbidden
Without advanced approval
Humour not encouraged, seen as a distraction
Offenders may be barred from further meetings
With a fined to be paid by himself and his Brown Duck
Brown Ducks only
Thoroughly checked for false colouring
Ducks not oversize or underweight
Ducks will be disqualified for flying, swimming or running
Walking only permitted
One mile to the finish
Winning Duck recorded by Brown Duck judge
Winning Duck will lead a walk past with all the other Ducks
Past the chairman of the Brown Duck fellowship
So ends another successful day
Of the Brown Ducks annual depressing day, enjoyed by all except the Brown Ducks.

The Bearded Mountain People

The bearded mountain people arrive with their wives, family friends and supporters
For their annual festival of bearded fashion
When the winter snow melted off the mountains
After a long hard winter
To prepare and style their beards
For their all important day
High quality beards only, open to both men and women
False beards will be disqualified and sent back up the mountain unable to join in the
fun and will receive a 2 year ban
On discretion of the tug master
Appointed by the judges to tug at the beards
Some animals will be invited to take part
In the animal section
Mountain goats, donkeys and some dogs
Brown bears not included
Have their own festival
Winning beards will have a photo shot and their photos on the club wall.

The Bell Rang

The bell rang on dreamer's hill
Where the old man of the river stood
Care not for love he said
A smile given
As he stood with his walking boots in hand
Cooling his hot summer feet in the fresh water stream that flows to the Dove
His dog named flash sits and waits with a gently tail swish keeping the river flies off
his wet nose
While over head the birds fly up and about in the blue cloudless sky
Not so the man on dreamer's hill when the bell rings loud and clear will soon be on
his way up river to his Fisherman's hut
And on the way with flash his trusted dog will sing his rendition of care not for love
on dreamer's hill give a smile and shout when the bell rings out
A fisherman yes a wife has not in his mildew hut he lives alone with his dog named
flash and the sound of the bell on dreamer's hill.

The Biscuit Boys

The Biscuit boys are back in town
Shouting, kicking bins, punching the air
They have arrived, dive for cover
Shouting howling singing out of tune
It's their version of the world cup
Can they get hurt?
No they are immune to pain
Head and body scars to prove it
Town folk have to leave the street
Shutters down
Run for cover
Fear is their game, they like it that way
Until the blue lights arrive
To practice their truncheon skills on what they call wooden heads
Not that the Biscuit boys are worried its part of their night out
The one with the most bruises buys the first round
After another encounter with the blue lights who also enjoy themselves drumming
on wooden heads
They crawled their way home
Biscuit boys, Biscuit boys, poor Biscuit boys, the town folk are relieved
Until they return again for another Biscuit boy show.

The Blue Goose Fair

The blue nose man
In the corner with a can
Had no room to hang his blue feathered hat
While he counted his pennies
For the blue feathered goose man's fair
Who arrived for the annual, not advertised
Passed on by word of mouth by goose to goose
Only blue gooses and blue feather hats are allowed to take part
With their owners
Gate entrance pennies only accepted
The blue nose man in the corner smiled to himself
With his goose sitting in his blue feathered hat
His blue goose washed and shampooed in his farmyard water trough
And a song was sung at the Blue Goose Inn
By each blue goose with their owners and blue nose himself with another can in
hand sang his of rendition of The Old Blue Hat to his beloved blue goose
And all the blue feathered hats joined in
While at the same time they were all counting their pennies and each blue feathered
goose helping out and blue nose himself fell asleep and his goose in his hat and woke
when the fair was all over without spending one penny

The Cabbage Eater

I was having my glass of beer as I normally do in my local pub and through the corner of my eye I notice a strange fellow walking around, I had a strange feeling that he was going to slot in near me, he looked an odd type of fellow one of these guys who was going to say something, I could sense it and then he spoke.

He said, "Do you like cabbage?"

I said, "Yes, sometimes, not all the time."

Then he said, "I like cabbage, I'm a cabbage eater, had a bowl of cabbage for my breakfast this morning." And I said to myself, "What's coming next?"

Then he said, "I come from a family of cabbage eaters when we're all together we get stuck into bowls of boiled cabbage."

Then he said, "I buy ten heads of cabbage each week."

Then I said to myself, "This is a weird guy."

Then he said, "I make clothes out of cabbage leaves, trousers, coats and hats."

I said to him, "How long do they last?"

He said, "I get three days out of them. I don't wear them outside, they're for my own private use, all my family make clothes out of cabbage leaves," he said, "would you like to come to a cabbage dinner?"

By now I'd experienced cabbage sickness. I thought to myself, "I better not insult him by saying I don't really like cabbage that much, for this fellow is a fanatical cabbage eater." I thanked him and told him that I was off green vegetables for the time being, doctor's orders as I might have a problem with my stomach, I will if he doesn't stop talking about cabbage. He said he was sorry for me, I was more sorry for myself listening to him, he could not stop talking about cabbage. I couldn't get away from him as he bought me another drink.

He told me his name was Charlie and proceeded to tell about his wonderful recent cabbage party with family and friends.

The Donegal Fair

It's a long way to the Donegal fair
With my fair haired lady and my bottle of beer
A feather in my hat my fiddle on my back
We danced to the tune of Donegal Moon
On the road we came from Glenties town
We waved goodbye to our friends and all
We sang our song as we pass Kilrean
The weather was good the air was fresh
I smoked my pipe along the way
At the Donegal fair my fiddle I played
Everyone danced the craic was good
My lady fair up she stood and sang her favourite rendition
My Sweet Old Donegal everyone clapped and asked for more
While I smoked my pipe and drank more beer we danced and sang
the night away The morning came we waved goodbye
to our friends and all at the Donegal fair
On the long road back we sang our song and danced to the tune of
the Donegal Moon
Goodbye good day to the Donegal fair with my fair haired lady and
my fiddle on my back and my bottle beer is not coming back.

The Man From Clare

Kitty O Leary met a strange man
On the road to the pig mans fair
Can you dance a fine jig with a man from Clare
By the light of the silvery moon
With my fiddle and pig
And the goose on the loose
And a comb for my blue brown hair
Indeed you're a strange man with your fiddle and pig
And a goose on the loose
On the way to the pig mans fair
To dance a fine jig
With my welly boots on
Could damage your blue suede shoes
Worry not my dear with your nut brown hair
And my pony tail to match
You're the right girl for a man from Clare
To dance by the light of the moon
With your welly boots on
And my blue suede shoes
And a fiddle without bending my bow
So Kitty O Leary danced a fine jig
With a man and his pig from Clare
And a goose on the loose
Came to join in the fun
On the road to the pig man's fare
And they danced all night till the sun came up
Then parted without saying a word
And so ends the tail of the man from Clare
With his fiddle, pig and goose
O Leary went back to her worried husband
Who wondered what the fuss was about
On the road to the pig man's fare.

The Mildew Hut

He who walks unnoticed
Finds himself alone
Steady careful under foot
And sun rays over the hilltops
And misty colours
Filter over summer hedge groves
Where hedge sparrows
Dance in and out with the sun rays
And he listens to the new awakening
Birds already breakfast eating
His leather boots are in tune with the dawn chorus
Against the gravel path that leads to the old fisher mans hut
Now covered in moss and rot
That's his retreat from reality
Where he hangs his hat and his mind
Memories are fading fast he knows full well
Yet a glint in his bloodshot eyes
It's not all what it seems to be
For he can visit his youth
Or any part of his long history
Yet all gone
He can look out at the fresh water river
As it flows by
The river never gets old
It has total long life
That's the answer he thought
Go with the river
He can't swim
Look at the moorhens they don't swim they float
Don't try it old fisherman
I know what you're thinking
Just sit in your mildew hut
And listen to the sounds of yesterday
And maybe tomorrow may never come for you.

The Millwheel Turns Again

The millwheel is turning
Who's yelling and shouting
The cattle are grazing the farm boy is sleeping
Wake him and tell him his not dreaming
The millwheel is turning and graining again
Excitement is growing chickens are clucking
The farm boy is hollowing
Five long years the millwheel stopped working
No graining no flour to bake the bread
The farm boy arrived dancing and singing
To the beat of the millwheel turning
How did it start
Billy the squirrel remembered
Where he hid his nuts five long years ago
And jammed the millwheel
And now he has retrieved them from the millwheel
And all the farm yard folk with their animals danced around the millwheel
As the farm boy sang his happy rendition of the millwheel is turning free again
And Billy squirrel promised he will be careful where he buries his nuts in future
The farm boy thanked Billy squirrel for remembering and sang he's a jolly good
squirrel and all the farmyard folk and their animals joined in too.

The Old Road

I rambled round the old road
Where I wondered so long ago
Where I first met my true love
friends and neighbours too
We parted with tears my true love said will I return again?
I would return my dearest love
Those words faded throughout the years
Where has my true love gone with my friends and neighbours too?
To land so far away
And now a stranger in my land
And strangers they are too.

The Open Road Festival

Shabby Bert stood to show off his not so new green threadbare suit
To his good friend waistcoat Bill who had arrived for the eagerly awaited annual men
and women of the open road festival held once a year near the old town rubbish tip
with a clearing for the event
You look well in your not so new green threadbare suit said waistcoat Bill to his
friend shabby Bert and myself in my inside out not so new blue yellow waistcoat I
found in my park bench basket
Thanks waistcoat Bill I found my suit on dead Billy the fox no use to the dead
thought I though it fitted me better than dead Billy the fox
It's a tribute to the memory of Billy the fox that his suit is going to the festival and
together the two friends journeyed on to the festival to meet all their friend's of the
open road who converge from all over the country
And all will remember the sad loss of poor Billy the fox and a great show of thanks
to Shabby Bert although Billy the fox is not with us for this year's festival his suit is
here instead and they all danced the gipsy farewell around the campfire burn to the
memory of late Billy the fox
The festival was another great success for the three day event of dancing singing
story telling joyful banter by the men and women of the open road
And Shabby Bert and his friend waistcoat Bill waved goodbye to all their friends and
agreed that this year's festival was the best as they all headed home along to the wide
open road that's their home.

The Redundant Family Chair

Broken damp mildew chair
Outside never again inside looking out
Many who sat looking out
Are outside never again inside looking out
History
Old chair played its part
Young grew old on family chair
Now they're outside
Only the chair is looking in now
Demolition underway
Chair sitting on top of rubbish truck
Goodbye chair
Outside inside rubbish dump
Looking out from under the rubbish tip.

The Reluctant Pig and Goose

Around the bend near Hillmans Hill
Came uncles Ted and Ed
To the market fair they are under way for a sale or two maybe
With their reluctant pig and goose in tow who are not ready for the chop or the pot
Uncles Ted and Ed understand their demise and insured them they have come of age
and ready to stand in the market day sale for a butcher or two maybe
And stand they have in the market sale ring and bought and saved from the chop or
the pot by a family for their animal farmyard retreat
Uncles Ted and Ed said goodbye to their pig and goose with a smile a nod a profit
made to their home near Hillmans Hill without their reluctant pig and goose in tow.

The Shoemaker King

Come to the palace
And see the new king
Tim Tack they call him
The shoemaker king
On a throne made gold
He sits with a smile
Stitching and fixing
And sewing with style
Humming away to the tune of the lute
While mending and bending the leather to suit
His people sit watching
Amazed with delight
There sovereign of shoes a ruler so rare
Proud of their king they declare him the best
Tim Tack they call him
The shoemaker king.

The Toothless Sailor

The toothless sailor woke up from his drunken slumber
Half buried beneath the wet morning sand
With a crab fastened to his cauliflower ear
Shaking the sand off himself
And wiping his bloodshot eyes
He shouted who pinched my half bottle of rum
And my tobacco pouch
My shipmates have gone
And left me buried in the sand with a crab for an earring
After we had danced the horn pipe and sang the Jolly Roger
Oh dear what can I do
Serves you right cried the squeaky old crow
High up in his crow's nest lookout
Your ship has gone and left you shipwrecked in the sand
Not so sure of yourself squeaky old crow
This sailor is not done for yet
You think a pirate? Yes I may be
Before we danced and drank our rum
I buried a bag of gold in the sand
Filled the other bag with sand
So my shipmates have gone off with the wrong bag
And I will dance a crow's nest horn pipe
And sing a shipmates farewell.

Too Many Years

Look at you through too many years
You're teeth shades are grey like your hair
On your back sits a clown
Loud sniggers and all
His past it, he's over the top
Faded away with mildew decay
Washed up in some bone yards retreat
Replaced in the rain
Revive on a crane
Held high and over the top
You're finished you're scrapped
Retire while you're old
Hand over and make way for the lost
Time is not your friend
Against you it stands
It found you while you were still young not old
Except the things you cannot change its over and done your finished your gone wake
up you might find it's only a dream
Relief yes for a time till you open your eyes and find you have already retired.

Trail Dweller

Going south my love, the night time trail dweller,
Dips his desert hat shows off his red boots to match the red desert sand,
And forward goes a true son of the red desert sand,
Who claims to be the great desert sandman,
The only survivor of the turn of the century great sandstorm,
Found buried ten feet under a sand dune by a friendly scorpion,
Tells his sand story wherever he goes,
Whoever cares to listen to his tail and buy him a pint or two,
At his local sandstone bar and happy if you offer another pint or two to give his
rendition of his camel song out of tune which he blames the sand in his lungs his
girlfriend agrees with a nod or two, she's well trained thought
Some of the locales and the sandman dips his hat and agrees.

Trumpet Blues

Harry Trumpet lost his trumpet
Near the old Trumpet Bridge
Into the river his trumpet did fall
Poor Harry cried and sneezed
Which sounded like his trumpet blues
On his trumpet blue nose
His father Billy Trumpet
Found Harry's trumpet while fishing on the River Trumpet
Which cheered Harry up
So he could play his trumpet blues again
On his trumpet not on his blue trumpet nose.

Upside Down Paper Reader

He who reads his daily newspaper upside down
A view with a difference
A new way of looking at the news
Gives the rest of his body equal rights to his head
A true pioneer of body rights
Not just about print
About words less important
When you realise how much you have missed out on news with a view
That could influence your life
Better if you stand on your head without your glasses
Hanging on your nose
Which would get in your way
While you're making paper planes
When you're finished reading upside down your daily newspaper
Take a photo of yourself before It's too late
You might go dizzy when the blood flows to your head
Which would confuse the news
It's all about making a difference upside down and downside up
Looking up not looking down.

Where the Jacks

Myself alone somewhere quiet
Moments of peace without concern, spaced out
Someone's space
Whose space
Wake you're back again
Without a light
Without an open door closed
Out in the cold night air
Two makes one
World and me uncertain
Listen to yourself when you're wrong so what
Dance if you can, without your shoes
Or your socks if they smell
Like your breath
Where's your teeth
In the bone yard retreat
Stand back not to far you might fall down
Or into the canal again
Too many cans over and out
Where's the Jacks.

Who's in Who's Out

He walked in She walked out
He walked out She walked in
In out what's it all about who's in who's out
The Cat's going out the Dog's coming in
The Dog's going out the Cat's going in
Nanny walking in Granddad walking out
Granddad walked in Nanny walked out
In out what's it all about who's coming in who's going out
Who finds it usually not the Parrot or the house Mouse who are more settled then
the house people or there Cat or Dog
Which makes no sense to close the open front door always in use never closed
What's it all about the neighbours may ask or any other nosey parkers who
happened to notice as they pass by
The house people with their Cat and Dog are pleased they have been noticed
Maybe that's the answer they are attention seeking the Parrot and the house mouse
agrees and so does there nosey neighbours agree to disagree
And the insiders or outsides do not care less who agrees or disagrees
They will continue their great family tradition of who's going out and who's coming
in.

Wilson Picket

Wilson Picket old time dancer,
Stood on a nail and found no answer,
Eat a hamper like a camper, joined the army with some laughter,
Joined the navy and found a baby lost without a proper name,
Found the mother in a cornfield looking for her new born child,
Became a hero of the nation left the navy and welcomed home,
Wilson Picket returned to dancing found a partner and settled down.

Wonder No More

I wonder, I wonder, I wonder no more
Through highways and byways I wonder no more
Love never held me and why should it be
And time did I live for
Yet time passed me by
Yesterday's memories are lost in the past
In the wind and rain where seasons bring change
Yet a journey man's life is a different lament
When leaves on the trees are found on the ground
Seasons may change love comes and goes
Where people remembered soon to depart
Where the wise and the wearier pass by in a hurry
And love never found me and why should it be
And time did I live for yet time passed me by
Look at the free bird high on the wing
On the highway of life it's never the same
Where yesterdays are gone and tomorrows come and go
And memories remembered until dust came to stay
And time did I live for yet time passed me by.

Woodland Fair

The gentle breeze blew back her hair,
Revealed her soft brown eyes,
What beauty shone from one so fair
At our woodland annual fair,
From where she came with such a glow never have I seen before,
While the fiddler played our gypsy's songs she danced a step or two,
Around the leafy carpet floor, what grace what charm I cannot hide
Captivated my mind's eye view,
While sun rays danced weaved its way through autumn woodland trees
And we all join in the gypsy two step dance around we went
Our eyes met smiles exchanged and all the time she danced
In our circle a call for a song to be sung up she stood to sing her rendition of
A wondering dancing gypsy love song while the fiddler played the wonderful
haunting melody we all clapped and shouted for more many more songs were sung
as our day wore on and my gypsy love disappeared from out sight
Only memories remain of my gypsy Queen at our woodland annual fair.

Yellow Feather

Look at the feather,
The bright yellow feather,
That blow through the window,
To land on the bed near the farm boy pillow,
Who had come from the meadow when the leaves turned yellow,
The same as the bird who has shed his feather,
To grow a new feather a bright yellow feather,
For the summer meadow that will be yellow.